The Rich, the Poor — and the Bible

How hard it is for those who have riches
to enter the kingdom of God!

Luke 18:24

THE RICH, THE POOR—
AND THE BIBLE

By
CONRAD BOERMA

THE WESTMINSTER PRESS
Philadelphia

Translated by John Bowden from the Dutch
Kan ook een rijke zalig worden?
Een onderzoek naar bijbelse gegevens over arm en rijk

© Ten Have, Baarn 1978

Translation © John Bowden 1979
First published in English 1979
by SCM Press Ltd, London,
under the title *Rich Man, Poor Man — and the Bible*

Published by The Westminster Press ®
Philadelphia, Pennsylvania

PRINTED IN THE UNITED STATES OF AMERICA
9 8 7 6 5 4 3 2 1

Library of Congress Cataloging in Publication Data

Boerma, Conrad.
  The rich, the poor — and the Bible.

  Translation of Kan ook een rijke zalig worden?
  British ed. published in 1979 under title: Rich man,
poor man — and the Bible.
  Includes index.
  1. Poverty in the Bible. 2. Wealth — Biblical
teaching. I. Title.
BS680.P47B6313   1980   261.8′5   80-15337
ISBN 0-664-24349-5

Publisher's Note

This book by Conrad Boerma, published originally in Holland and translated in Great Britain, provokes serious thought and discussion wherever it is read. In offering it to an American audience where it might be a resource for study in classes and small groups in churches, the Westminster Press has provided, as an aid to discussion, "Study Suggestions" beginning on page 99.

795/

Contents

1

The Bible: A Strategy for Change

I would not have written this book if I did not believe that the Bible has important things to tell us, not only about spiritual matters but also about material concerns. Even so, when it comes to the question of poverty and riches, the Bible might not seem to have very much to offer. After all, revolutionaries and counter-revolutionaries both seem to find it easy to support their position from the Bible, with the same ease and apparently the same justification. Either side can discover a congenial text to give extra authority to a political or social standpoint which has already been adopted for other reasons. For example, when President Marcos declared a state of emergency in the Philippines on 21 September 1973, claiming all authority for himself and destroying the last remnants of democracy, a traditional picture of Jesus was shown on television with a voice in the background saying, 'I have come not to abolish the Law but to fulfil it.' That is a quotation from the gospel of Matthew (5.17).

Anyone who begins to study those parts of the Bible which deal with poverty and riches will come up against what at first sight seems to be a confusing amount of contradictory material. At first riches are a blessing, but later they become a curse; at times poverty seems to be praised, but elsewhere it is regarded as a disgrace. Moreover, sometimes poverty and riches seem to have a spiritual significance, whereas other passages are connected with a particular social situation. Sayings like 'Blessed are you poor' (Luke 6.20); 'In the world you have tribulation; but be of good cheer' (John 16.33); 'My kingship is not from the world' (John

1

18.36); 'What does it profit a man, to gain the whole world?' (Mark 8.36) and many others seem to make light of real poverty by putting all the emphasis on poverty as a spiritual problem. By contrast, other texts, above all in the prophets, are concerned with material poverty.

The same kind of confusion can be found in theological interpretation. One of the standard works on poverty in the Bible, by the French Roman Catholic A. Gélin, has an appendix giving a historical survey of biblical interpretation since 1882.[1] He reviews thirty-nine books in all. It seems that in 1882 people were principally interested in poverty as a religious question. Later on, however, interpreters came to lay considerable stress on poverty as an economic and social problem. As a result, the same term can have widely differing meanings, and there is every chance that the biblical material will be distorted. In fact it often transpires that the Bible is misused in two ways when it is brought into discussions about the problem of poverty.

This happens first when material poverty is made light of, with reference to the spiritual significance of poverty (which it can sometimes have), and when answers are sought on a materialistic level to problems which are non-materialistic, often with reference to the same biblical evidence. One example of this is the view that we should be concerned with technological progress because that is *the* solution to all kinds of problems, or that the question of poverty will be solved when people in developing countries are able to share in our Western prosperity.

Some forms of Marxism also have a tendency to present exclusively materialistic solutions to spiritual questions. However, there is more to man than what he eats. (And those who want to interpret this text – cf. Matt. 6.25; Luke 12.23 – in an exclusively spiritual sense should emphasize the word 'more'.)[2]

Obviously, the terms used in the Bible cannot be detached from their social and political background; in this respect they are part of a historical process. Consequently it is wrong to wrench biblical texts out of their original setting, rather than reading them against the background of their time.

2

It is all the more important to approach the question in this way because there is clearly an underlying connection between poverty and riches. Poverty and riches are not independent phenomena. One person is poor because another is rich. Poverty is not a state of deprivation which has come about by chance; it is a result of the richness of the rich. And nowadays the rich no longer ask the poor, 'Why are you so poor?' The poor ask the rich with increasing urgency, 'Why are you so rich?' We would be right in detecting a note of recrimination here. Poverty is no accident; it is determined by the structures of society.[3]

A critical investigation of the biblical material is concerned with these very structures.

However, we may well ask whether the biblical writers noticed the structures themselves. Were they aware of the way in which the relationship between rich and poor affects the development of the society in which they live? Did they see the intrinsic structural connection between poverty and riches? And what did they actually do? Did they accept the poverty of some people and the riches of others? Did they offer help and consolation? Did they seek structural solutions? Did they acquiesce in the situation? In short, how did they react to all these phenomena?

In the rest of the book I shall try to find some answers to these questions. It will emerge that the biblical writers were preoccupied with them in many different ways; they sought a variety of solutions and pointed to a variety of different expedients.

Those who speak to us from the Bible were children of their time and their surroundings. It makes a considerable difference whether poverty is considered by people from court circles, taking their life of luxury for granted (as happens in the wisdom literature), or whether it is considered by people who have been in its grip and have experienced the humiliation which it brings. A man is what he says. We can also see how the Bible gives divergent answers. It does not offer any simple solution to the problem. It adopts a variety of approaches. Sometimes the same words acquire different meanings which can even prove contradictory.

However, we can discover some lines of development. Trends

emerge, pointers can be seen; opposition movements arise to combat deterioration in the situation. I shall attempt to describe these opposition movements and to draw conclusions from them. Interpreters have always tried to take account of the historical and cultural background in their exegesis of the biblical texts. When we are dealing with terms like riches and poverty, with all the nuances which have become attached to them in the course of time, it is all the more necessary to pay attention to who says what, where, and to whom. At this point the political background should not be overlooked. People like Belo and Rostagno[4] have made an important contribution in their special preoccupation with an investigation of these background questions. Such 'political interpretation' has been described as 'an interpretative method that uses the tools of historical materialism and which, starting from analysis of the modes of production and the class conflicts resulting from them, leads us to understand the events of the New Testament as an expression of this historic dialectic.'[5]

Like any other, this method too can lead to abuse. One's own perspective can be so coloured that texts are simply used to bolster up one's own prejudices. The political interpretation of biblical texts can serve as a justification for political choices which have already been made and are already established.

However, that is true of any form of exegesis. No exegesis can be objective. Still, anyone who takes account of these dangers will find it nothing but gain to include the social and political background in his investigation and to clarify the structure of the society in which the text was written. In this way it is possible to demonstrate the social significance of a text and to draw parallels with our own social situation. That is the point when one-sided texts can show their strength. We are not concerned with a sophisticated approach in which the truth lies somewhere in the middle and can amount to almost anything. If the texts about riches and poverty can mean what we want them to, then anyone can disclaim responsibility and put off the poor with a pious ideology or romanticized words of comfort. The important thing is to be ready, after careful and obedient attention to all the

4

biblical evidence, to choose that part of the truth which is relevant at a particular moment and which in all its one-sidedness demands to be applied to a particular situation. The one truth of the Bible is concrete, and therefore by definition one-sided.

Anyone who tries to read the Bible in this way runs risks. But they are less than the risk we run from a Bible that can mean anything. If the Bible can mean anything we like when it comes to specific questions, it in fact means nothing. And too many people are already finding that this is the case.

In the rest of the book I shall try to do more than play one text off against another. I shall attempt to find a strategy for change which is rooted in the biblical tradition. This change is urgently needed as long as world resources are still distributed in so grossly inhuman a way and there is so little political concern to give up existing privileges. Change is needed not only in world conditions, but also within our own country. Prosperity is unjustly distributed, and the forces arrayed against a more equitable distribution of income are strong. It is easy to see how our social system, despite all its welfare measures, continues to stimulate the urge to acquire more without taking account of those who are hurt in the process.

That is true of society as such, and even the church itself is extremely conformist in this respect. Not only do church boundaries sometimes seem to follow the contours of social classes, but even within a church, mutual solidarity or brotherhood stops at the pay packet, or at least passes it by. Despite all its splendid provisions for service and all its good intentions, as far as I know the church has never made proposals for transforming its spiritual fellowship into a sharing of material goods.

Tertullian, who was born about AD 160, could still say, 'All things are common among us but our wives.' The *Didache*, The Teaching of the Twelve Apostles, still argued for common possessions. 'For if you have what is eternal in common, how much more should you have what is transient?'

This question cannot be avoided. It arises out of the very real fellowship to be found in the Christian community in the first centuries, the roots of which go back to the time described in the earliest books of the Bible, when the question of poverty and riches began to be a problem.

The question continues to crop up right through the Bible and therefore needs to be kept on the church's agenda permanently, as contemporary discussions show all too clearly.

2

Rich and Poor: Social Developments in the Bible

Words in the Bible

The Bible has a large vocabulary for describing the poor man and his situation. This fact alone indicates the attention paid by the biblical authors to the question of poverty. However, the meaning of particular words does not always remain the same. It shifts as the situation develops and changes.

In the Old Testament, the commonest word for 'poor' is *ani*: it is used seventy-seven times, and above all in the Psalms (twenty-nine times). Literally, it might be said to denote a person who is bowed down, who occupies a lowly position. He has to look up to others who are higher than he.

The *ani* is the man who is bowed down under pressure and finds himself in a dependent relationship. Spanish has a word which describes this condition well: it talks of the *humilhados*, the humiliated, who can no longer stand upright because of economic and social pressure. It is clearly a term which describes a relationship, though it is striking that the *ani* is not contrasted with the rich, but with the man of violence, the oppressor, who puts the *ani* in his lowly position and keeps him there. This contrast is significant.

The word *anaw* is very closely associated with *ani*. Although the terms are sometimes used interchangeably, *anaw* tends to be less materialistic. The *anaw* is the man who knows himself to be of little account (before God); he is humble or gentle. Here the emphasis can be more on poverty as a spiritual attitude. The word appears eighteen times, eleven of them in the Psalms.

The word *dal* is used above all for physical weakness and

material poverty with no other connotations. For example, Pharaoh's cows in Gen. 41.19f. are *dal*. The Jewish peasants were called the *dalat ha'arets*.

The word *ebyon* occurs a great many times (sixty). It is the designation for a man who finds himself asking. He can ask in two senses: from other men, as a beggar, and from God.[1]

In the Bible, all these words have an emotive connotation. They are not neutral descriptions,[2] but indicate circumstances which urgently call for change. Right at the end of the Old Testament a neutral term appears: *rūsh*, the needy. The verb *rūsh* means 'to be poor'. It is striking that this more neutral word is never used by the prophets. All the words mentioned above appear in a single sentence in Amos 2.6f. (with the exception of *rūsh* – but Amos, after all, is a prophet): 'Because they sell the righteous (*tsaddiq*) for money and the needy (*ebyon*) for a pair of shoes; they that trample the head of the poor (*dallim*) and turn aside the way of the afflicted (*anawim*).'

This quotation also makes it clear that Amos is certainly not concerned to describe poverty as a neutral condition. This is further confirmed by the fact that he puts the poor on the same footing as the righteous. For Amos, being poor is comparable with being righteous. I shall return to this parallel in more detail at a later stage.

The New Testament also has different words for describing the poor man and his condition. *Ptōchos* is the commonest of them.[3] Like *ani*, it derives from a verb that means to duck away (in fear). The *ptōchos* is the type of man who has to try to live completely without means and is therefore reduced to begging in order to stay alive. His life is dependent on the help of others. He is reduced to charity. There is also the *penēs*. The *penēs* is the poor man who has to struggle hard to keep his head above water. The *ptōchos* is the marginal man. It is his fate to have nothing, just as it is the fate of the *penēs* to have to live frugally.

Sometimes the *penēs* is idealized: he is the industrious countryman. The *penēs* is the respectable poor man. The *ptōchos* is not. All he can do is to hold out his hand.

8

In ancient Greece the *ptōchos* was the despised beggar who hung on as a parasite in the homes of the rich and the noble. He did not deserve any pity (Greek did not even have a word for it). The only chance of some sympathy was if anyone who had originally been rich suffered misfortune and then had to go round begging. The classical example of this is Odysseus in Homer (see *Odyssey* 21.327).

The god of the Greeks is certainly on the side of the stranger, but he is never the protector of the beggar. By contrast, Jesus declares that it is the *ptōchoi* who are blessed.

In addition to *ptōchos* and *penēs*, biblical Greek has a variety of words to describe the poor and poverty: the lowly, the needy, the insignificant, the weak, the simple, the oppressed. All these words tend to run into one another. The Hebrew words were translated into Greek in very different ways. Their content also changes. Sometimes they have negative connotations and sometimes positive.

In itself, a list of words does not say very much. The great variety of terms and expressions can show how precisely the Bible noted and registered poverty. We can see the poor man with a bent back and hands held out, and observe something of the degeneration of that time. But the words keep changing. The same terms sometimes even acquire opposite meanings.

That is also clear from the way in which words for rich are used. The Old Testament has a variety of expressions: riches, influence, power, possessions, abundance, nobility, pre-eminence.

The same is true of the New Testament. The most important word is *ploutos*, which means something like full, much. To be rich is to have an existence which is full of good things, where there are no shortages. As a result it can be called happy and blessed. But here too, a word which is in itself positive can become the opposite, as is the case with the words which describe being poor. Poverty can be negative, but in another instance it can be positive: for example when the word is used to describe humility. The term rich can be used as a taunt, but at the same time it can be an indication of happiness and blessing.

9

The Septuagint, the Greek translation of the Old Testament, therefore finds it impossible to render one Hebrew word consistently by the same Greek term. Because of this, we need to look for the background from which these words get their real content and against which they change their meaning.

From Abraham to the settlement in Canaan

The first thing to notice is that the question of poverty and riches seems hardly to play any significant role at all in earlier biblical literature. One indication of this is the number of times that the word 'riches' is used:

Six times in the Pentateuch (the first five books of the Old Testament)

Nine times in Joshua and Judges

Twenty-three times in the later 'historical' books

Thirty-four times in the prophets (no less than nineteen times in Isaiah)

Ninety-three times in the wisdom literature (including Jesus Sirach)

Sixty-nine times in the New Testament.

The word 'poor' does not occur at all in the book of Genesis. There are famines (Gen. 12.10; Gen. 41). Prosperity is by no means universal. Life is hard and callous. But there is no question of a contrast between the rich and the poor, and we saw that this contrast is the main feature of the terms. Where there is talk of riches, for example in the story of Jacob's meeting with his father-in-law Laban (Gen. 30), these riches consist of possessions: 'large flocks, maidservants and menservants, and camels and asses' (Gen. 30.43).

Such wealth is certainly not a private possession. It is the wealth of the tribe or of the family. Riches which can be accumulated from plunder in war, from presents or through skill (or in the case of Jacob, through trickery), are a sign of God's blessing, a gift of God. As Deuteronomy 28.1–14 will put it at a much later stage, it is the 'reward for obeying the voice of the Lord your God' and 'being careful to do his commandments'. Indeed, in the stories about Jacob everything is not black and white. For all his craftiness, Jacob does not prove wholly successful. While his cunning is marvelled at, it is also mocked. The change from astute Jacob to limping Israel called for more than the manipulation of the laws of heredity by means of which Jacob was able to increase his flocks. It needed a nocturnal struggle with the angel of the Lord: that struggle was what made Jacob, and his people, into Israel (Gen. 32.22–32).

Riches are really no problem in the first books of the Bible. The essential feature in biblical thought at that time is that riches are a consequence of observing God's law. In Greek thought riches are a consequence of craft and slyness. The gods are on the side of the cunning.[4]

In biblical thought, riches are initially success guaranteed by God to those who observe the laws of the covenant. Abraham is the living example of this unproblematical view of riches. His possessions are sheer blessing. The righteous prosper. Abraham is the type and the representative of the view that obedience in faith leads to prosperity. This approach can be traced right through the Old Testament. There is a healthy sense that listening to God's commandments is a very useful occupation both for oneself and for society. This is expressed very clearly in the blessing which is attached to the fifth commandment: 'that it may go well with you' (Deut. 5.16; cf. Ex. 20.12). The sign of peace and prosperity is that everyone should be able to sit quietly under his vine or fig tree without anyone making him afraid (I Kings 4.25; Micah 4.4).

Now it is worth noting that in this phase of Hebrew history, the patriarchal period, possessions are never a privilege obtained at the expense of others within a particular environment. Possessions are the riches of the semi-nomadic tribe or of the tribal alliance, and everyone within the tribal alliance profits from the prosperity of the tribe. If one man is rich, all the members of the tribe are rich.

In nomadic times there was probably not even a word for 'poor'.

The word *ebyon* seems to be of non-Israelite origin; it is used for the first time in the Book of the Covenant (probably the oldest part of the Bible: Ex. 20.22–23.33).[5]

It is presumably no coincidence that the term 'poor' appears here for the first time. For this was the very point at which the social structure of the people of Israel was modified. There was an end to nomadic life. Israelites became farmers, and began to settle and to change the proportion of their possessions.

Before the settlement in Canaan there seem to have been no clear distinctions between poor and rich. We hear of a certain solidarity within the social group as a whole. True, there is a distinction between poor and rich. There are male and female slaves, the vanquished and the vanquishers. But this evidently raised no social problems. At least they were not experienced and criticized as such. Within the tribe there are no economic conflicts and no social classes. Even the slaves do not pose one. They are part of the family. The family is a financial unit (cf. Lev. 27).

According to one scholar, the fifth commandment is meant to preserve this unity. The elderly, who had little economic contribution to make, must nevertheless continue to be revered.[6]

About 1200 BC a change took place. At that point the Hebrew tribes broke away from their semi-nomadic existence. They settled and became farmers, tied to their land, and gradually took over the agricultural areas of Canaan. Before this period, at the time of Abraham and his descendants, there is no mention of property. In the end, the only piece of land which the wealthy Abraham owned was a burial place for his wife Sarai. He had to pay a good deal for it. It was 'the cave of the field of Machpelah east of Mamre (that is, Hebron) in the land of Canaan' (Gen. 23.19). Otherwise Abraham, for all his possessions and riches, remained 'a stranger and a sojourner' (Gen. 23.4). Stranger and sojourner are still meant literally here. The terms were used later by David in a religious sense (stranger and sojourner with God, see I Chron. 29.15; Ps. 39.13). Here too, though, they were still bound up with the material possessions of the patriarchs (see also Heb. 11.13). The development is comparable with that which takes place over the term poor. To begin with the term has a purely material reference, but later it acquires a spiritual connotation.

This sense of being a stranger was further heightened when the Israelites prospered in Egypt, though they seem to have obtained some land there (see Gen. 47.11). In Egypt all the land was the property of Pharaoh or of the temple.[7] In other countries around Israel, like Mesopotamia, land was for the most part in the hands of the king; the rest was owned by communities, families or private individuals. The king presented some of his land to vassals who later handed it down as a legacy. Israel never knew such a feudal system. Time and again it was stressed that the Holy Land is 'the Lord's possession' (Josh. 22.19 and various other passages). Israel should really be described in terms of a theocratic feudal structure, in which God is the liege lord.

From bad to worse in the promised land

To begin with, when the tribes of Israel settled in the land of Canaan round about 1200 BC, they occupied the less fertile hill country, and from there slowly extended their sphere of influence in the direction of the plains. The books of Joshua and Judges suggest that this may not have been very easy for some groups. Joshua 21.43 reports that the whole country is in Israelite possession, but in Judges 1 that only seems to have been the case with certain regions. Slowly but surely – and this is the problem in the book of Judges – the tribes came under the influence of the Canaanite-Philistine system of values. The Philistines and other groups had migrated to Canaan in the first half of the twelfth century BC and had continued and strengthened the political system already existing.

The land was divided into units, each with a city at its centre and with a prince as ruler. Well-known centres in the old Canaanite city-state system are Gaza, Ashkelon, Ashdod and Gath. It was in this period that the Israelites entered Canaan tribe by tribe, and took possession of the less fertile hill-country. For the time being the tribes still occupied separate areas. In fact, for a considerable period they continued to live among the non-Israelites.

There they encountered a military culture which was alien to their experience as desert people. They themselves were not akin to the much more aggressive camel nomads; they were nomads who travelled around and settled where the pastures proved suitable; later they would move on elsewhere. They were afraid of cities and chariots.

De Vaux[8] describes how all Bedouins believe themselves to be a cut above settled farmers, precisely because there are no social classes in their tribes. Even slaves are members of the family. Similarly, the word Canaanite continues to have a negative connotation throughout the Old Testament. For example, in Gen. 9.20–27 it is Ham who dishonours his father Noah (v. 22), whereas Ham's son Canaan is the one who is cursed (v. 25). The repetitions in vv. 25, 26, 27, are worth noting: 'and let Canaan be his slave'. Here 'Canaan' is clearly a taunt.

Later on, the name continues to have an association with city culture, sacred prostitution, the cults of Baal and Astarte and with trade and industry in a negative sense. Well on into the Old Testament, merchants and traders are called Canaanites, sometimes in a neutral sense (Isa. 23.8; Prov. 31.24; Job 40.25), sometimes as a taunt (Zeph. 1.11, 'traders').

In the Authorized Version, the promise of salvation in the last sentences of the book of Zechariah (14.21) runs: 'there shall no more be a Canaanite in the house of the Lord of hosts'; the New English Bible translates it, 'no trader shall again be seen in the house of the Lord', which puts this promise in a very different light. It could well be that in John 2.16, 'You shall not make my Father's house a house of trade', Jesus was thinking of this latter meaning.

It is clear that two value systems clashed from the moment when Israel began to settle in Canaan. This clash is the theme of the books of Joshua and Judges, and they describe the tension that results. It was a struggle to preserve the values of the earlier way of life in the face of adaptation to the Canaanite life-style.[9]

14

The principle of solidarity which characterized Israel was markedly strengthened by Moses' lawgiving. As Gélin points out in his book about the poor in Israel, Moses had created a communal spirit and kind of collective sense.[10]

The settlement of the Israelites in Canaan brought these values under strong pressure. From being semi-nomads, the Israelites turned into small independent farmers, each of whom owned a small piece of ground. They became rivals, albeit in family groups, as a result of changing fortunes brought about by better or worse harvests. Anyone who was given a bad piece of land to begin with soon became poor and was compelled to sell himself and his family into slavery.

The system of values changed even more quickly as men married into Canaanite families which were more skilled at agriculture. The possession of property became the centre of interest. People began to want to increase their possessions and become rich. The tenth commandment, which derives from this period, expressly forbids the coveting of land, wife or possessions (cf. Ex. 20.17; Micah 2.2; Deut. 5.21).

The basis of social life was not the tribe but the family, the *mispahah*, which was established in a city or a village. At this time a distinction arose between the poor and those who owned land. To be poor is not to have (or no longer to have) land. The development of an economy involving dealings in trade and land disrupted the equality of families. Some families became very rich and others slowly became poor. Two trends developed within society: an aristocratic tradition centred on the cities and a prophetic tradition based on the covenant.

We must therefore conclude that, even in the Bible, poverty is directly connected with the structures within which men live.

Poverty does not develop of its own accord. People do not become poor because they are idle; they become idle because they are poor. Nor is the problem created by an anti-social attitude or any other kind of negative attitude on the part of the poor man; it is that the social and economic situation has changed and the semi-nomadic people of God have come to grips with an agrarian culture based on individual or family possessions. It is worth noting that in all the texts from this period, in both the Pentateuch and the prophets, the poor man himself is never seen as the cause of poverty. Only in the later literature, in Proverbs and Ecclesiastes, is the poor man blamed for his poverty, and in any case these books derive from court circles.

This means that solving the problem is never a matter for the poor man; it is the task of the rich. The rich man is reminded of his responsibility and, to an increasing degree, of his guilt. He must transform his social success into a blessing for his fellow-countrymen; he must be the one who encourages opposition to the widening gap between rich and poor. However, he fails to do this.

In reality, for all the public criticism made by the prophets and in spite of legislation, the social development continued, and the gulf widened further.

The influence of the army

The chief factor in this negative development seems to have been the way in which Israel gradually began to follow the Philistine pattern of forming an army. When they arrived in Canaan, the Israelites had some political and administrative organization, but for the time being it was not centralized and it was certainly not monarchical. Authority rested with the elders, who were more or less subject to the control of a popular assembly of all able-bodied men. Apart from the fact that women were not represented, this gathering seems almost democratic. When the son of the great judge Gideon, a certain Abimelech, wanted to become king in Canaanite style, he was criticized very sharply. One need only read Jotham's famous fable in Judges 9.

Gradually, however, the military build-up by the Philistines began to leave its mark on Israel. The organization of the Philistine city-state seems to have been less important than the effective military machine which they controlled. The Israelites were not a match for this professional army. Israel had a kind of conscript army with a charismatic leader, a judge, at its head. However, this was not up to coping with the far superior Philistine force which extended its power in all directions. The cry for a real king became louder and louder. Samuel yielded, with considerable reservations (I Sam. 8), and Saul, the first king, lost no time in forming his own military group (see I Sam. 14.52b; 22.6; 18.13). Because his authority was still that of a charismatic leader, in most respects, the situation had not yet changed radically.

From a military point of view Saul's army was a great success, but it introduced an alien element into the new kingdom of Israel. Israel's unity came under threat, and a dangerous internal tension developed within the apparatus of state. In Edom and Moab, Israel's neighbouring countries, hereditary dynasties came into being. These came increasingly to be regarded as models and indeed as necessary political instruments. So on the death of Saul, and the defeat of his popular militia, the people were confronted with a choice. They could either fall back on the old system of more or less independent tribes, a kind of tribal federation, with every prospect of being controlled or dominated by the Philistines, or they could continue further with the development of central state control.

David (1000 BC) chose the latter course. He set up a professional army, consisting of Cherethites and Pelethites, with which he managed finally to overthrow the Philistines. At the same time, however, he broke up the old tribal system and created a kingdom, annexing territory and drawing up boundaries; establishing spheres of influence; creating a diplomatic service, choosing a capital and introducing other elements which hitherto had been alien to Israel. Moreover, the monarchy now came to rest in the hands of one family. Under David, what had hitherto been a pattern of charismatic leadership, with a leader elected by the people or appointed by God (i.e. chosen by lot), now became a hereditary monarchy.

In I Kings 1.35 David appoints his son Solomon *nagid*, prince. Hitherto this right had been reserved for God alone, as is evident from the way in which the ruler was anointed by priest or prophet.

The Israelite popular assembly served to ratify such a decision. David appropriated the right to himself. Solomon continued this centralized approach. He enlisted forced labour to build the Temple (I Kings 5.13; cf. also I Kings 15.22) as a substitute for the old system of drawing upon the tribes for manpower. In this way, a special class of officials came into being alongside the military, with their own particular privileges (cf. I Sam. 8.11–18; I Sam. 22.7). The king himself became increasingly powerful and emphatically came to dominate and control the economy. The subject was increasingly called upon to serve the king rather than vice versa. Solomon's trading enterprises were clearly set up as a royal monopoly.

From the time that Israel settled in Canaan, property became less and less communal and more the possession of private individuals or families. To begin with, the differences between rich and poor had developed more or less by chance. Now, however, these differences increased steadily through the development of the monarchy, which was regarded as a military necessity.

To use the terminology of the theory of dependence,[11] a centre of privileged people developed within the city, in contrast to a peripheral population settled in the country or on the edge of the city. These people had to provide goods and services for the court and court circles, and thus found their existence becoming increasingly marginal. They became poorer and poorer.

This negative development proceeded very rapidly, above all between 1000 and 800 BC. Special professions came into being in the city and round about the palace. Some people saw a chance of becoming great landowners. In times of crisis and war the most cunning or most 'fortunate' of them succeeded in enlarging their possessions quite considerably. The prophet Isaiah pronounces their own condemnation: 'Woe to those who join house to house, who add field to field, until there is no more room, and you are made to dwell alone in the midst of the land' (Isa. 5.8). They became increasingly remote from the country proletariat which they themselves had created.

The social climate changed. The frugal atmosphere of communal

18

life gave place to pomp and ceremony, with palaces and international alliances, in which trade, waging war and making treaties played a significant role. In both Judah and the kingdom of ten tribes (which arose in the ninth century as the result of a revolt against abuse of its privileges on the part of the royal house), there came into being a prosperous aristocracy, which contrasted markedly with an ever-increasing marginal population. The gulf between rich and poor became deeper. Whereas in the tenth century living standards were still more or less equal, very great differences were evident two centuries later. Excavations in Tirzah (*Tell el-Farah*) indicate that in the tenth century BC. all houses still had the same dimensions and furnishings. Excavations in the same city from the eighth century BC show that different districts had come into being: a well-to-do neighbourhood for the rich and slums for the poor. The one people had split up into different social groupings or classes. Poor and rich were in opposition.

Poverty as disgrace and exploitation

At this time there was a very important change in human relationships. The accent shifted. To begin with, poverty had still been a matter of economic inferiority, brought about through a setback or through other more or less chance factors. The poor man was not despised because of his poverty.

He 'only' had to be helped out of his poverty. Now, however, the rich began to treat the poor as though they belonged to a lower order. Because a person was poor, he became different, i.e. of lesser value. Poverty came to be seen as a symptom of a much deeper deficiency in a person. The poor began to be despised. They no longer counted. Because they were poor, they had fewer rights than others and less insight. The story of Nabal in I Samuel 25 illustrates this very clearly (see especially vv. 10f.). Nabal is the embodiment of the rich and haughty fool. When people ask for their due, he keeps them at arm's length with devastating remarks like, 'There are many servants nowadays who are breaking away from their masters' (v. 10). He refuses to look closely at what is happening and thinks only in general terms, disregarding the existence of people with names of their own ('Who is David? Who is the son of Jesse?'). The height of his shamelessness is that he regards people who have no lodgings and no fixed address as idlers, and treats them accordingly. The writer of this story registers very critically the climate within which the poor have to live.

In Ecclesiastes 9.13–15 we have an engaging little story which also shows clearly how it is the poor man who is not credited with any insight: 'There was a little city with few men in it; and a great king came against it and besieged it, building great siege-works against it. But there was found in it a poor wise man, and he by his wisdom delivered the city. Yet no one remembered that poor man. But I say that wisdom is better than might, though the poor man's wisdom is despised, and his words are not heeded.'

It is also clear from this critical story how the increase of social distinctions had other consequences. As well as being poor, the poor man is trapped, oppressed and exploited; because he is poor, he is also inferior.

Being poor becomes synonymous with being oppressed. The poor man is caught in a vicious circle which can be broken only by the attitudes and actions of the rich, but that never happens.

The relationship between rich and poor becomes more complicated. It is a matter of cause and effect: you are poor because he is rich; and at the same time, because you are poor you become even more so. You belong to the dregs of society, to a lower class – and no one listens to you. 'To be poor' and 'to be oppressed' amount to the same thing. The standard expression, 'who oppress the poor' (Amos 4.1; Prov. 14.31; 22.16; 28.3; Zech. 7.10; Psalms 72.4) attributes the cause of poverty to the rich. The poor man is oppressed, and the cause of this oppression is the rich oppressor. This is very clearly the case in passages like Isa. 5.8; Amos 3.9; Jer. 5.27; 6.6; 22.13; 22.17; Ezek. 45.9; Micah 2.1; 6.10; Hab. 2.9; Mal. 3.5.

'But you have eyes and heart only for your dishonest gain, for shedding innocent blood, and for practising oppression and violence,' says Jeremiah of his king Jehoiakim (Jer. 22.17).

From Old to New Testament times

The exile of the people of Israel in the sixth century BC may have made radical changes in national life, but it did not affect socio-economic relationships in any material way. The basic structure remained the same. Even after the return, there were still rich and poor, those with possessions and those without. Before the exile, the reformation under king Josiah (about 620 BC) was an attempt at renewal on the basis of the Torah with a view to calling a halt to this development. However, it did not meet with much success. There were certainly opposition movements (see the following chapters), but the basic economic pattern stayed the same. Structurally, everything remained as it was. From the social tensions which emerge at this time it is clear that the nature of the social problem was emphatically understood. This was certainly the case in the Hellenistic period after Alexander the Great. The coming of the Romans did not bring about any improvement here. The masses lived in fearful poverty. They were oppressed from two directions.

They had to fulfil their religious obligations. Even the sabbath year (about which we shall have more to say later) was turned upside down. The law relating to it was meant to protect the poor by compelling the great landowners to let their harvest stand once every seven years. This law was now also applied to people who could not live off their land. And at the same time they had to pay the normal temple taxes.

In addition, the Romans taxed them. This taxation could amount to a quarter of the harvest. If they were forced to borrow, the interest charged put them in a hopeless situation. This produced a displaced urban proletariat. There were no strikes; but bands of men were often formed to get what they could out of the situation. Some of these bands, like the Maccabees and Zealots, even engaged in armed rebellion.

The vocabulary of the New Testament teems with references to the social conditions of the time. There is talk of landowners, tax-collectors, labourers, slaves, honest and dishonest stewards,

21

creditors, unjust judges and widows who plead in vain for their rights. It is all reminiscent of a feudal atmosphere.

Among the poor there was a strong feeling of hostility towards the ruling party. When Jewish rebels took over Jerusalem in AD 66 from their base in the Temple, the first thing that they did was to burn the city archives. The land registry and the register of debts went up in flames. At the same time, all the slaves were freed. The rebellion was actively supported by the poor and the young. The rich, even the rich Jews, continued to back the authority of Rome.

Among the Jews scattered over the world in the Diaspora, in the period after the destruction of the second Temple in AD 70, the relationship between rich and poor can best be described in a simile used at the time. It was like that between wolf and lamb.

There was a ruling Jewish 'class', consisting of the high priestly families (and the Sadducees), the great landowners, businessmen and the court circles around Herod and his senior officials. They profited from collaboration and from keeping in with the occupying forces. In the rebellion mentioned above, the Zealots did more than burn the archives; they also killed the high priest Annas and other notable figures.

This tension between a rich upper class and the masses is characteristic of the whole of the Roman empire. Poverty was a gigantic problem, especially in a capital like Rome. The authorities tried to keep the masses quiet by government regulations. There were distributions of grain and distractions were provided by bread and circuses. Under Julius Caesar and Augustus, around the beginning of the Christian era, between 150,000 and 200,000 unemployed people in Rome had to live on the dole.

All the time, this process of concentrating power in a few hands continued. The influence of the state was extended. The republic, intended as a *res publica*, a concern of the people, became an empire, an *imperium*, with a widespread network of roads planned for trade and communication, controlled by an army with bases everywhere. A small number of rich individuals stood out from masses who were on the breadline: slaves, the unemployed, beggars, and impoverished peasant farmers. These were dependent on the dole, on the tranquillizers distributed by the government, or on the charity of the rich. They sat even at the gates of the Temple and looked for alms. Their only hope seemed to be those who were sympathetic to them (cf. Acts 3.1–10. But see also pp. 83f.).

Summary

I hope that it has become clear from what I have said so far that in Israel poverty is very closely associated with the economic system in which people live. When Israel gave up its life in the wilderness, and a semi-nomadic people became a nation of farmers, men acquired private possessions and poverty emerged as a social problem. Social tensions increased as a result of the development of the army and the monarchy along lines parallel to the pattern among neighbouring peoples. Different social groups came into being with conflicting interests. Slowly but surely, poverty ceased to be a purely material circumstance and was seen as a sign of inferiority. It was experienced as exploitation. To an increasing degree, the poor man became the victim of oppressors. The Bible makes this problem very clear. In this way the rich became the target of the most important counter-attack on unjust conditions: prophetic criticism.

Many writers in the Bible wrestle with the question of poverty. They do so for different reasons and from different perspectives which we shall consider more closely in later chapters. As a result of this, poverty becomes a concept with a wide variety of meanings and nuances. It can be an objective description of a particular situation: the harvest has failed, and next year the poor man will have to work extra hard just to get by. However, the word increasingly comes to denote someone who has suffered hurt. The poor man is the man without rights, the man who no longer has any value. He becomes a victim. And at this point those who actively believe in the covenant God make a strong protest. The provisions of the Torah have been violated.

Others continued to expel the poor from society. The poor man is despised because he is to blame for what he is (as a result of his idleness). This development can also be traced in theological terms. Since riches are a blessing, poverty must be a curse. Men bring down the curse on themselves. The book of Job is written as a protest against this theme.

These developments continue above all in the later books of the Old Testament, especially in the wisdom literature. True, there are also social protests, but the general view is that poverty overtakes a man because he is idle. The writer C. van Leeuwen put it this way: the condemnation of poverty and manual labour by the authors represented in the Israelite wisdom literature betrays their origin in the well-to-do strata of society, in this case in the court circles.[12] The same is true of Egypt.

The wisdom literature accepted the fact that society was divided into different social strata. Unlike the prophets, the authors do not see this division as the result of injustice: it is a consequence of destiny (God) and human action. This connection between destiny and action can be seen above all in the book of Proverbs.

Job questions the connection. Among his speeches we find acute descriptions of poverty, which is also presented as oppression:

Men remove landmarks;
    they seize flocks and pasture them.
They drive away the ass of the fatherless:
    they take the widow's ox for a pledge.
They thrust the poor off the road;
    the poor of the earth all hide themselves.
Behold, like wild asses in the desert
    they go forth to their toil,
seeking prey in the wilderness
    as food for their children.
They gather their fodder in the field
    and they glean the vineyard of the wicked man.
They lie all night naked, without clothing,
    and have no covering in the cold.

They are wet with the rain of the mountains,
  and cling to the rock for want of shelter.
There are those who snatch the fatherless child from the breast,
  and take in pledge the infant of the poor.
They go about naked, without clothing;
  hungry, they carry the sheaves;
among the olive rows of the wicked they make oil;
  they tread the wine presses, but suffer thirst.
From out of the city the dying groan,
  and the soul of the wounded cries for help;
yet God pays no attention to their prayer.   (Job 24.2–12)

However, the theological view that poverty is man's own fault persists. On the whole the rabbis had a negative view of poverty. Under Herod, the Pharisees parted company more and more from the mass of the population. It is better to suffer than to be poor, one of them wrote. The poor man was compared with the leper, the blind, the childless, even with the dead. Poverty is a curse.

In one development, then, poverty was seen as shame and guilt. By contrast, there was a completely different view which was prompted above all by the psalms. God is the one who takes the side of the poor. In one sense he identifies himself with them. In this way the poor man becomes the pious man. He has a firm place in the cultic psalms as the one who is protected by God. In the pre-exilic royal psalms (Ps. 72; 132), the king champions them in God's name. The poor man (always in the singular) is contrasted with those who work unrighteousness (always in the plural). The poor man acquires a particular aura of his own. He becomes more or less the authentic man. Because the rich man is the oppressor, the poor man is seen increasingly as the righteous one. He is the real man of faith. In texts like Isa. 29.19, the pious man is clearly equated with the poor man. 'The meek shall obtain fresh joy in the Lord, and the poor among men shall exult in the Holy One of Israel' (see also Isa. 32.7; Zeph. 3.12; Zech. 11.11). 'Poor' becomes 'pious', and the slave can become the suffering servant of the Lord.

All the words with which the Old Testament so accurately

25

describes the poor become a subordinate part of the vocabulary of a theology of grace. Poverty becomes a word with spiritual connotations. There are profound associations with the God of Israel, his law and his love. However, this awareness is never developed into a system. In the exile it is never said, 'Salvation is on the way because now (at last) the people are in a(n ideal) state of poverty.' The mood is very volatile and never bécomes concrete.

Of course, a theological approach develops for which poverty now is a prelude to riches in the future. The future must make up for the present and restore a proper balance. Those who are rich in this world will be poor in the next; and those who are poor in this world will be rich in the next, say the Essenes (150 BC–AD 70).

In the New Testament period there is a confusing wealth of theological explanations, solutions, clarifications and protests. Consequently it is not surprising that during an Assembly of the Dutch Reformed Church in the autumn of 1977, when there was a discussion about possibilities for a new life style, a wide variety of biblical conceptions appeared one after the other. References came thick and fast: to advice from Proverbs to enjoy the world; to Paul's view that the time was short (eschatological relativism); to the rich young man who went away sorrowing; to the thousand-year kingdom; to a belief in catastrophe thought to be implied in the Revelation of John; to doubt whether our society can be improved; to exhortations to revolution, and so on. The very variety of these references made one thing certain. No one could change anyone else's mind, so in fact nothing happened. About a week later, in a Bible study, I was told that 'the rich and the poor together' (Prov. 22.2) was a reference to a future meeting in heaven; until then they would have to go their separate ways.

In the following chapters I have tried to collect together some of the solutions to be found in the Bible and to describe them more closely as protests against the widening of the gulf between poor and rich. Generally speaking, we find three trends which exist side by side and complement one another.

3

The Fight against Poverty

So far we have been looking at what the Bible says about poverty against the background of developments in the Old Testament period. I have tried to be as objective as I can, but complete objectivity is really impossible. The Bible never gives simply a description of poverty. Those whose words we read there are extraordinarily concerned about poverty; they are cross, they get worked up, they refuse to accept it, they complain, they protest, they look for ways out. Theirs is not an academic interest in the phenomenon of the relationship between poor and rich. They see real people succumb to poverty; see them trapped, threatened and oppressed. They are personally involved in the questions they raise and are certainly not objective or detached. Sometimes this does not make it very easy for those of us who read their words at a much later date. We do not know precisely what they are talking about, what the conditions were and what caused them. And it depends to some degree on our particular perspective how we arrange the evidence and what lessons we think we can learn from it for our own time.

However, anyone who reads the Bible will be impressed by the fact that poverty is never taken for granted. No one is satisfied with the conflicts between groups of people. In all kinds of ways, the biblical authors are concerned to help the poor and to fight against poverty.

We have already seen that this happens in the Bible from different perspectives and in different ways. That, too, does not make it any easier to chart developments or classify different

27

approaches. An attempt was made as early as 1924 by the German theologian H. Bruppacher. In his book on the Old Testament view of poverty, he makes a distinction between three assessments of poverty in the Bible: as laziness, destiny and oppression. He is well aware that distinctions of this kind can be dangerous. It is possible to use one argument (poverty is laziness) to rob another argument (poverty is the result of oppression) of its force. And it is very dangerous indeed to talk of poverty as destiny. In that case it is God's business, and we can wash our hands of it. The Bible singles out injustice and oppression as the two principal causes of poverty. Bruppacher's important conclusion is that in the Old Testament we find 'an enormous shift in causation. The Bible indicates that sin, rather than nature or an evil fate, is the cause of poverty. No distant alien power is made responsible for the harsh conditions under which some men suffer, but their neighbours, the members of their own people.' This was Bruppacher's outspoken judgment at a time when theology was very much concerned with the social question.

Some time after the Second World War, this view was revived. The French Roman Catholic theologian A. Gélin also attempted a classification of the biblical evidence in his book *Les pauvres que Dieu aime* (The Poor whom God Loves), published in 1967. He made a distinction between (i) poverty as a *disgrace*: a scandalous state which should not occur in Israel, and in which the poor man is a victim; (ii) poverty as *sin*: because riches are God's blessing, poverty must be a curse and the poor man must himself be a sinner; (iii) poverty as *piety*: 'pauvre' (poor) becomes 'pieux' (pious); because God is close to the poor, the poor must automatically be close to God.

These meanings, with all kinds of nuances, are certainly to be found in the biblical texts. But because Gélin lumps them together unhistorically, apart from their social and economic background, the chance of improper use of the evidence and general confusion is very great. Gustavo Gutierrez, one of the most distinguished Roman Catholic advocates of liberation theology, rightly criticizes this confusion in the last chapter of his famous book *Theology of*

28

Liberation.[1] In this way poverty is spiritualized far too easily and made to look attractive, a tendency which recurs today when the poor man is seen as the true representative of humanity.

The Peruvian theologian Gutierrez himself describes poverty in the Bible as a scandalous condition (*estado escandaloso*), and as spiritual childhood (*infancia espiritual*); this leads him to propose his twofold model for action: solidarity and protest.

He rightly links the description of poverty in the Bible with our own action. This is correct for two reasons. First, because the Bible itself makes the connection. Poverty is never described calmly; it is challenged. The poor man is comforted or encouraged; his oppressor is accused. In short – something is done about poverty. From the beginning it is opposed. In the Bible poverty is never accepted; it is challenged at a variety of points. Secondly, Gutierrez is correct because reading the Bible is meant to prompt us to some action. It stimulates our critical sense, gives us something to think about and inspires us to effort, and prevents us from being complacent. Reading the Bible is more dangerous than we often would like it to be. It puts us under an obligation.

That does not mean that we can follow the Bible in a simplistic way. The Bible does not gives us a blueprint. From within their own social situation its authors described how God changed their world, how he took the side of the poor and championed their cause. From within this tradition we, too, can try to do the same thing in our world; we can look for the will of the same God; seek possible parallels; and join the same resistance movement against poverty and its causes.

It has become clear from the previous chapters that poverty is never an isolated phenomenon. It is closely connected with the social framework of a society. In Israel, poverty first emerged as a problem when social conditions began to change, at the time of the settlement in Canaan. From that moment, various attempts were made in Israel to counteract this generally disastrous development. The poor were not the only victims; at the same time the rich were preparing for their own downfall.

The counter-attack came from several sides. In fact it was one opposition movement against the social and economic trends of the time developed on a broad front. However, the variety within it was so great that at first sight it might seem as though trends in the movement clashed with one another or cancelled one another out. This has been a common reaction: every heretic finds a text to his liking, and even worse, every oppressor finds a text to give an aura of biblical respectability to his standpoint. However, that is merely a superficial impression. Opposition to poverty in the Bible is on a large scale: it is really there, even if it can never be summed up under a single heading. Centuries of experience, countless disappointments and minor successes, produced the complex evidence.

Broadly speaking, I would describe the opposition to poverty in the Bible in terms of three movements:

1. Opposition to poverty through social structures. The characteristic biblical word for this is righteousness.

2. Opposition to poverty through the community as the people of God. The characteristic word for this is solidarity. (In fact the Bible uses the term brotherhood, but I have preferred solidarity, in order to make it clear that sisters are also included in this brotherhood.)

3. Opposition to poverty through the self-confidence of the poor man himself. The characteristic word for this is spirituality. (I have preferred this difficult word so as to make it clear that the vital factor here is God's spirit and his inspiration. I have tried to include under this heading the ideas of the poor man as the pious man and of poverty as spiritual childhood.)

All these developments begin in the Old Testament and go through into the New Testament, with various shifts in emphasis. The three opposition movements sometimes seem to clash with one another. Some details may appear contradictory, but essentially they make up a coherent pattern. They are complementary. They represent the different fronts on which the one war was waged: the war against injustice and inhumanity and against that disintegration of society which goes by the name of poverty.

4

Poverty and Social Structures:
The Demand for Righteousness

The Law

The Torah, the Jewish Law, contains the guidelines for the freedom which God has given his people. It is more than a collection of regulations; it also includes legends and historical accounts. For Jews, the Torah, the first five books of the Christian Bible, was supplemented and commented on by the 'former prophets' – what we know as the historical books (Joshua to Kings). Most scholars believe that the oldest written part of the Torah, which developed into its present form over many centuries, is the so-called Book of the Covenant. This comprises the text of Exodus from 20.22 to 23.33. In the Book of the Covenant we can read regulations about worship; a discussion of the rights of Hebrew slaves; and rules relating to the life and property of neighbours. Particular attention is paid not only to slaves, but to all kinds of people in need of help: strangers, widows, orphans, the poor (Ex. 22.21–27; 23.1–12).

These texts probably come from the time when the people of Israel was settling in Canaan. Structures changed, and some groups were in danger of becoming victims of this change. As soon as that happened, prophetic criticism of the Canaanite way of life began: not just in general terms, with empty phrases, but with specific proposals. Hebrews who had become impoverished as a result of disasters, and had to sell themselves as slaves to secure their livelihood, were not abandoned to their fate; after serving for six years they were to be allowed to return to society as free men (Ex. 21.2ff.). Kidnapping men to sell as slaves seems still to have been practised at that time. According to some scholars, the eighth commandment, 'You shall not steal', primarily meant 'You shall not steal a man'. In the Book of the Covenant such kidnapping is expressly prohibited and punishable with death (Ex. 21.16).

The Book of the Covenant contains the well-known words 'life for life, eye for eye, tooth for tooth, hand for hand, foot for foot, burn for burn, wound for wound, stripe for stripe'. As so-called civilized people we find this positively crude, but the regulation was in fact meant as a curb on excessive use of force. Lamech boasts: 'I have slain a man for wounding me, a young man for striking me. If Cain is avenged sevenfold, truly Lamech seventy-seven fold' (Gen. 4.23f.). The rule of an eye for eye is an improvement on this vindictiveness based on brute force. Throughout, the Book of the Covenant has a very strong sense of equality and calls for its permanent restoration. The texts convey a feeling of respect for human dignity. Strangers, widows and orphans are not to be oppressed. God will avenge them.

It is in this Book of the Covenant that the word 'poor' appears for the first time in the Bible. 'If you lend money to any of my people with you who is poor, you shall not be to him as a creditor, and you shall not exact interest from him' (Ex. 22.25).[1] 'You shall not pervert the justice due to your poor in his suit' (Ex. 23.6). He is not to be treated harshly. God is gracious (Ex. 22.27).

This book also contains the first mention of the rule that land is to lie fallow in the seventh year (Ex. 23.11); it is presented again in much more detail in Lev. 25.1–7, where the period is called the sabbath year. The reason behind this rest for the land is a concern for the poor (and the cattle): 'so that the poor among your people may eat'. At a later stage (Deut. 15.2), remission of debts is substituted for the fallow year. By then land and goods are evidently no longer the only form of possessions; debts can be settled by other kinds of payment.

In addition to the Book of the Covenant there are various other legal regulations which aim at helping the poor. The ten commandments are directed against a concern to accumulate possessions.

32

In the tenth commandment, covetousness is singled out for special mention. There is an interesting difference in the way in which it begins in the two variant forms of the commandments which have come down to us. In Ex. 20.17 there is no mention of coveting one's neighbour's field; the commandment begins with a prohibition against coveting his house. In Deut. 5.21, house and field appear side by side, and the first prohibition is against coveting one's neighbour's wife. The social climate has obviously changed.

Social conditions themselves are discussed in the laws for the sabbath year (Lev. 25.1-7) and the year of jubilee (Lev, 25.27; Num. 36.4). As is already clear from the Book of the Covenant, in the sabbath year, once every seven years, the produce of the land was put at the disposal of the poor. The year of jubilee is even more radical. Once every fifty years all slaves have to be freed. Property acquired by anyone had to be returned to the original owner. In that year all debts had to be remitted. Nowadays we would call these measures structural solutions. They not only take account of the need but restore just conditions.

Release from debt and slavery and some redistribution of the means of production are the radical measures commanded by the Law. It is questionable whether a complete restoration of original equality is envisaged here. In any case, however, poverty is not only made tolerable but tackled at its roots – indeed at the most important point of all, the question of property. The Indian economist G. T. Kurien once said that Karl Marx was so influential because he tackled this very problem. It is one which the church will not be able to avoid much longer.

The whole of the book of Deuteronomy, which many scholars date in the time of Josiah's reformation (620 BC), but which in any case goes back to much earlier sources like the Book of the Covenant, is impressive evidence of strong opposition to developments in society which put human relationships in second place.

It is uncertain how far these laws were actually put into practice. According to the Greek Jewish writer Flavius Josephus, who lived in the second half of the first century AD, the sabbath year was certainly observed. How strictly it was observed varied from one place to another, but even the Greek and Roman authorities took it into account. At the request of the high priest, Alexander the Great granted the Jews exemption from taxes every seventh year. Julius Caesar did the same thing. Soon after the destruction of the Second Temple (AD 70), however, the law proved impracticable. The economic depression was so deep and taxation had become so high that it could not be continued. Incidentally, this law (the *shemittah*, or year of release) is still observed even now, to a greater or lesser degree, in some Jewish circles. The next year of release will be in 1979/80, or the year 5740 according to Jewish reckoning.[2]

It is more questionable whether the regulations about the sabbath year did much for the poor. As a consequence of the taxation imposed by Herod and his sons, and by the Roman authorities, at the time of Jesus most farmers had lost their independence. They lived almost like slaves. Their poverty was further increased by absentee landlords who worked through intermediaries, like stewards. Of course, they too wanted their share. The regulations for the sabbath year were an extra burden on these small farmers, who were already living in deep debt.

The year of jubilee probably remained a dead letter. De Vaux calls it a late and vain attempt to make the law of the sabbath year more radical by extending it to property. It remained a utopian law. Still, it is a very interesting one. No such legislation is known among any other people. It reflects something of the ancient Israelite idea of the people as one family and of possessions as common property. Laws of this kind kept alive opposition to the forces of self-interest and attempts to increase possessions at the expense of others.

The year of jubilee is the most radical attempt in the Torah to arrive at a fundamental redistribution of the means of production. It is a sign of outspoken criticism of a society which reserved the ideal of all Israelites, sitting at peace under a vine or a fig tree, as a privilege for the few. In this legislation, prophetic criticism was transformed into practical rules, concerned with living in accordance with God's will. The authors of the Bible make it clear that life as God wills it must be lived out in the context of a real society. This is the face which Israel must present to other nations, as the people of God.

The motive behind this legislation is not what has aptly been described as a wilderness mysticism, as though nomadic life itself was so ideal that it should now be given legal status. The wilderness was not particularly pleasant for the Israelites. It is the place of desperadoes and the home of demons (Isa. 13.21; 34.11–15). It is the barren land to which the scapegoat takes Israel's sins (Lev. 16). To have to wander through it as a nomad was thought to be a curse. This can be seen from the story of Cain and Abel. Cain the farmer is condemned to a wandering nomadic life after he has killed his brother.[3]

True, nomadic life could provide an ideal, as is clear from groups like the Rechabites (Jer. 35), and later the Qumran sect. This ideal comes to the fore in certain sayings of prophets like Jeremiah (2.2), Hosea and Amos. However, Israel's past in the wilderness was never romanticized for its own sake. The prophets recalled the purity of Israel's original religious life and the purpose of the covenant. They are the guardians of the Mosaic system. Their criticism often seems revolutionary, but it is not. Like so many radicals, they refer back to the past. Consequently, some people even call the prophets reactionaries, because they no longer follow the predominant pattern. So the deepest motive behind the legislation is certainly not a wilderness mysticism. Still less is it the idea that material goods might be an evil in themselves. Prosperity, even material prosperity, the possibility of enjoying the good things of the earth, was seen and experienced as a blessing. It was a gift of God. Originally, prosperity and justice were connected. Only later (see Isa. 57.1) does the thought arise that the righteous man should expect suffering and poverty rather than prosperity.

Nowhere in the Bible is poverty an ideal, as it is with the later mystics. Nowhere is poverty glorified or romanticized (see e.g. Jer. 5.4, with its criticism of the lowly, 'because they do not know the way of the Lord, the law of their God', and Isa. 9.16, where even the fatherless and widows are included among the evildoers and the godless). The fact that the poor man is sometimes – and with increasing frequency – called righteous is not so much to his own credit; he is righteous because his oppressor is so terribly unrighteous. He is therefore righteous in comparison with his oppressor, who withholds his rights.

So the God of the Bible takes the side of the poor. He chooses his party. But although the Lord God takes the side of the poor, that does not mean that the poor man is closer to God, as S. Rostagno, an Italian Christian Socialist, points out. Were that the case, poverty would be almost sacred, and there would be no need to fight it. The scandal and godlessness of poverty would be camouflaged, and biblical indignation would give place to compassion or pious talk. 'It would become a game with words . . . and with people', as Gustavo Gutierrez puts it. Such a game has in fact been played right down to our own times. There are those who praise poverty and call the poor the true representatives of humanity without becoming poor themselves. They oppose participation in development and all kinds of aid on the grounds that this does not help (though just criticism may be possible and necessary). Such a 'rich theology', or rather, theology of the rich, stands in sharp cotnrast to the anger of the law and the prophets.

The riches of the earth are meant for all. Little headway can be made in this direction by facile commendations of the poor. Hence one can understand why people in developing countries mistrust the theology of the rich West, even when this claims to be very radical. They have some justification.[4]

The prophets

In addition to the criticism implicit in specific legislation, there is a direct attack on poverty from the prophets. They do not mince words about the rich. The rich are the enemies of the poor. They are godless, haters, persecutors, men of violence, plunderers, usurers. They fight the poor, lay in wait for them, catch them in a net, seize them in claws, traps or nets. They are like lions, snakes, adders; they are arrogant, full of vanity, and wicked. They have a high opinion of themselves; they are scornful and crafty; their mouth is full of curses.

This selection of epithets is by no means complete. We have already seen something of the multiplicity and variety of the vocabulary used to describe poverty. From these taunts and tirades we can now see how concerned the prophets were to make a fundamental criticism of socio-economic relationships. The fury of the prophets at what men have done to one another is expressed with impressive force and vivid imagery. They themselves must have lived very close to the poor.

The prophetic texts are not just descriptions of situations. Their vocabulary is loaded, and directed towards the guilty, who are mentioned by name. The blame lies with traders who exploit their customers (Hos. 12.8; Amos 8.5; Micah 6.10f.; Isa. 3.14; Jer. 5.27f.; 6.12); with corrupt judges (Amos 5.7; Jer. 22.13–17; Micah 3.9–11; Isa. 5.23; 10.12); the seizure of property (Micah 2.1–3; Ezek. 22.29; Hab. 2.5f.; see the story of Ahab and Naboth, I Kings 21). This criticism of the rich is continued in the New Testament, above all in Luke (6.24f.; 12.13–21; 16.19–31; 18.18–27) and James (2.5–9; 4.13–17; 5.1–6).

This, too, is merely a selection. Anyone who reads the psalms will find something of this kind on almost every page. It is exciting to see how the criticism of social and economic developments proceeds. As riches and possessions are concentrated in a few hands because of the increasing power and corruption of the monarchy and the growth of trade and commerce in the cities, making the countryside increasingly poor, criticism is directed more and more towards the rich as a *group*.

This brings us to the question whether it is possible to talk of a class struggle as early as this.

Class struggle?

In biblical times the poor certainly cannot be said to be a 'class', if by that we mean an organized class which fights for the interests of the group against those who stand in the way of them. The poor are weak precisely because they are left alone and stand by themselves. They are isolated individuals, and as such are defenceless. Some modern writers, like the well-known socialist biblical interpreter F. Belo, constantly talk of 'class', but they only use the term to denote a group of people who are in a particular social situation and occupy an isolated economic position.

It is therefore important to be quite clear what one means when using the word 'class'.

As conflict developed within Israel, the prophets attacked the rich very clearly as a group. In fact it is the rich who appear as a class fighting for their own interests and seeking to secure and expand those interests. They are referred to collectively as godless: Jer. 5.26 is a typical example: 'For wicked men are found among my people; they lurk like fowlers lying in wait. They set a trap; they catch men. Like a basket full of birds, their houses are full of treachery; therefore they have become great and rich. They have grown fat and sleek. They know no bounds in deeds of wickedness; they judge not with justice the cause of the fatherless, to make it prosper, and they do not defend the rights of the needy.'

Rich and godless are often parallel terms, cf. Isa. 53.9: 'They made his grave with the wicked, and with a rich man in his death.' The prophets' criticism is often directed against prosperous people in general (Ezek. 22.6–13; Amos 3.10; 5.7–12). That is also the case with the prophecies of disaster (Isa. 3.1; 3.16–4.1; Jer. 5.26–31; Ezek. 22.24–31; Micah 2.1–11). They will be destroyed along with the splendour of Jerusalem (Isa. 5.14); their riches will pass away (Isa. 29.5), etc.

The rich are also often addressed as a group in the New Testament. As with the prophets, this criticism is stereotyped and impersonal. It is not so much directed against particular rich individuals as against a group of people who have made themselves rich. Luke is the evangelist most concerned with questions of poverty and riches. In fact he is seldom concerned with riches as such, but with the rich man and his riches in a particular situation. For him these are indications of a particular mentality and a pattern of behaviour about which he is very negative. He sees how it is no good for the poor man who is the victim of such behaviour, or for the rich man who forfeits his humanity and the possibility of the gospel (see Luke 6.24; 8.14; 12.15, 21–23; 14.33; 16.10–12; 18.25; more moderately in 16.9; 18.27). Luke's concern is above all for those who are materially poor. His gospel begins the theme of rich and poor in the impressive Magnificat (Luke 1.46–55). Mary's hymn of praise, with its associations with Hannah's hymn from I Sam. 2.1–10, is the prelude to a gospel in which the arrogant, the powerful and the rich come under the criticism of the gospel and priority is given to the simple and the hungry. Luke can sum up the message of Jesus in these terms: the poor have the gospel preached to them. He quite emphatically follows the prophets (Isa. 61.1f.) in his answer to John the Baptist's question about who Jesus really is (Luke 7.22).

The letter of James is more occupied with questions of riches and poverty than most of the New Testament letters. James, too, is concerned with the rich as a group: 'Is it not the rich who oppress you?' (James 2.6; 5.1). Luke and James are the New Testament writers in whose works the words poor and rich occur most frequently. 'Rich' occurs twenty-eight times in the New Testament. Luke has it eleven times and James five; 'poor' occurs thirty-four times: ten times in Luke and four in James. The theme is also prominent in the book of Revelation. There, too, the rich and the powerful are seen as a 'class', e.g. Rev. 13.16. The whole book expresses radical opposition to the manipulation of power and riches. With an almost aggressive delight, the author pronounces the death penalty on the world of Roman capitalism and its state, the whore of Babylon (18.10), dominated by powerful merchants (18.23). They make the city a metropolis steeped in the blood of prophets and saints and of all who have been slain upon the earth (18.24).

Our conclusion is obvious. Both Old and New Testaments are characterized by a fundamental criticism of the rich as a group. The rich are also addressed collectively. We may even speak of them as a class, but it is much more questionable whether one can legitimately speak of a class struggle (see p. 57ff. below:' A Christian revolution?').

In any case, biblical criticism of the rich as a group is radical. Their riches are corrupt. They already have their consolation and their reward. They will simply be sent away and have little chance of entering the kingdom of God.

The heart of the criticism

If we try to describe this whole opposition movement in one word, we come up against the very basis of the existence of the people of Israel. This basis is the covenant, the new order of existence grounded in the Lord and established in the Law of Moses, which is against slavery, exploitation and alienation. The starting point for the ten commandments in Ex. 20 and Deut. 5 is given in the words 'I am the Lord your God who called you out of the land of Egypt'. In the New Testament this covenant was expressly accepted as a starting point in the ministry of Jesus: he restored its original aim and made it universal. The hallmark of the covenant was righteousness. Of course the relationship between rich and poor is only one element in this covenant. The covenant is concerned with more than that, or rather, the relationship between poor and rich is just one of the characteristics of the covenant, which cannot be isolated from the other elements. Like all the other elements in the covenant it is a part which can stand for the whole and sometimes in fact does so. That is very much the case with the relationship between rich and poor, hence the vehemence with which the Bible makes the point. Anyone who takes this foundation stone away from the Torah causes the whole structure to totter.

It is also why the whole of the gospel can be described as the gospel of the poor. Those who hunger, those who weep, according to Matt. 5.4,6 and Luke 6.21, are people in physical distress. 'It is this true people of God', says Herman Ridderbos, 'which is addressed in the beatitudes and to which the salvation of the kingdom is proclaimed as their due.'[5] This covenant may not be

40

broken. Israel must remember the covenant, i.e. understand what it means and live it out day by day.

A variety of arguments can be found in the Bible for doing away with the conflict between poor and rich.

Serving the Lord and possessing the land go together. The new land is and remains God's. It is 'the Lord's possession' (Josh. 22.19); 'the Lord's land' (Hos. 9.3; Ps. 85.2); 'Your (my) land' (Jer. 13.18; Ezek. 36.5). The Israelites had to fight for the land, but in the end it was given to them by lot, i.e. through God's mediation. Even then, families rather than private individuals came to own it. Those who were successful in drawing lots saw to it that their family possession remained intact, that is to say, did not pass over irrevocably into other hands (this is very clear in Lev. 25.23: 'The land shall not be sold in perpetuity'). Even after the apportionment of land (which in any case did not go as smoothly as Josh. 6–12 might suggest; compare Judges 1), certain essential means of production, like pastures and wells, remained in the hands of the community. So it is not for charitable motives that the prophets address the rich upper class. They do not ask for a collection: they do not ask the rich to allow some of their wealth to trickle down, as happens in the debate over development. They base their case on divine law. They take their stand on the covenant. Poverty is unjust, and those who remain rich are unrighteous. The verbs used in the Bible make misunderstanding impossible: exploit, oppress, use violence, practise injustice.

'Unlike Roman law, Israelite law never threatens those who will not pay their debts with imprisonment. In fact we discover the contrary: anyone who seizes an Israelite by force to make him a slave . . . must be put to death.'[6] In Israel, the central concept on which justice is based is that of righteousness, with all that the term conveys in the Bible. A righteous man is faithful and loyal to the obligations of the covenant under which he lives. Righteousness involves the fulfilment of mutual obligations. The God of Israel proves himself righteous in this way. He does what he says. That makes him the righteous one. Righteousness works in two

41

directions. Positively, it brings liberation to the righteous; negatively, it damns the godless. It is concerned with the rights of the poor, the widow, the fatherless and the Levite (who was assigned no territory of his own in the division of the promised land).

The law does not confine itself to the right to a human existence and personal freedom; it has a marked concern with property and the means of production. In the Bible, the more unjustly the poor man is treated, the more righteous he becomes. In a book like Amos, the poor man is almost identical with the righteous man. The downtrodden take over the role of judges and kings. Kings derive their power and function from their obligation to secure justice for those who have no helper. Because they fail here, the poor are their judges. They become righteous instead.

The Bible assumes that everyone has someone to stand up for him or her. The wife has a husband, the child has a father, and so on. Thus everyone lives within a covenant. Where there is no natural helper, as a result of sickness, disaster or death, the judge or the king has to fulfil this role. Should they fail, or refuse to act, the helpless rise up to judge them, and God takes over the role of the natural helper (see royal psalms like Psalm 72). The poor are therefore 'the people of God'; cf. Isa. 3.15: 'What do you mean by crushing my people?' We constantly find references to 'the wretched among my/his people'. Identification between the poor and the people of God is not complete, but the judicial principle is clear.

God's righteousness is demonstrated by the fact that he takes sides with the poor and stands up for them. The oppressed are his people, for whom he appears, and whose cause he espouses in solidarity. His Messiah will also bring righteousness (Isa. 11.4).

The prophets are not economists or political theorists. What they do is to illuminate specific relationships from their 'theological' insight, their understanding of the covenant. Consequently they cannot regard poverty as a destiny; or as a position of inferiority which has come about quite by chance; or as a consequence of laziness or pleasure-seeking. Poverty is injustice and a

42

breach of God's covenant caused by the greed of the rich. The strong and the powerful use their considerable resources (which they are best able to acquire), not to further relationships within which men are placed by God but in support of their own ends. In this way they violate God's law and his ordinances. They tear apart what is meant to be a unity. They create disaster. Thus poverty is injustice perpetrated by violence.

Jeremiah (22.15) also makes treatment of the poor a touchstone of a man's knowledge of God or his godlessness. Anyone who oppresses and robs the poor oppresses and robs God. In this respect, property is theft. This now classic saying, coined by the nineteenth-century Frenchman Pierre-Joseph Proudhon (La propriété c'est le vol), thus has its roots in the Old Testament. The feeling remained alive until well into the early church, as is clear from the way in which Clement of Alexandria (about AD 200) calls private property sin (*adikia*).

In the Bible, the right to property is subordinated to responsibility for the weak members of society, and furthermore, to their right to the means of production.

To regard property as a possession to be made use of without taking other peoples' rights into account is to ignore the biblical conviction that man is simply a steward of the goods of the earth. This idea is particularly marked in Deuteronomy and Isaiah. God is the creator of heaven and earth. He exercises lordship over the earth and retains control over its resources. This power of God is not confined within the boundaries of Canaan, but applies in principle to the whole world.

How much this is the case can be seen from the function of the Temple. God is immediately present there, so at the same time the Temple is the seat of justice. God the Lord is the saviour of the poor, their hope, their stronghold and their liberator. The Psalms give a clear idea of this, whether they are individual or communal hymns or laments. In worship the poor regained their rights. There at least God's order still prevailed, and the covenant was restored. It is even probable that the Temple was a sanctuary, a place where the oppressed could have tangible experience of God's care and compassion. It is therefore no chance that the Psalms have regularly been rediscovered in times of oppression.[7]

It is worth pointing out that within the context of the covenant, material concerns are never made light of or spiritualized. This reflects the nature of the covenant and the God of the covenant. For us Westerners, there is a difference between our relationships with one another and our relationship with God. It is common to talk of two tablets of the Law, one divine and one human. In the Bible, these aspects belong closely together. According to Jesus, they are even the same thing.

In the Old Testament, love is an all-embracing association 'of God and man, man and God, God and things, man and man, and man and things, in a burning desire for an intimate relationship'.[8] Law in the Old Testament is not concerned with an ideal, but with specific and functional regulations. And everything belongs together. Even nature protests against the violation of human rights. 'All the trees of the wood rejoice before the Lord, for he comes' (Ps. 92.12f.).

In the Bible, things hang together. To know God and to apply the law is one and the same thing. The Argentinian theologian J. M. Bonino has made a study of the text of Hosea 4.6: 'My people are destroyed for lack of knowledge.' This is not intellectual knowledge, but knowledge of God. Those who know God walk in his ways. Obedience is not just a fruit of the knowledge of God; in certain cases it is the knowledge of God itself.[9]

Distinctions cannot be made between faith and love, action and prayer, horizontal and vertical: these terms are mutually interchangeable. Despite the variation in them they are fundamentally the same. The prophetic protest is permeated by this fundamental unity. For the God of the covenant, everything holds together. As Jesus will say in the New Testament: you cannot serve God and mammon (Matt. 6.24; Luke 16.13). If you try, there will be a lie in your existence, and God's people will vanish from the world stage.

The Old Testament thus launches a vigorous attack on the negative consequences of the history of Israel. With great élan, profound biblical insights, and from a radical tradition, the law and the prophets are advocates of the joy and the freedom of the covenant. With grief and anger they see how economic development, the expansion of the monarchy and the growth of a military complex disrupt the connection between love and justice and God and neighbour and material things. There is something tragic about this protest by the law and the prophets. In fact, they find it hard to apply their clear insight into such connections, to the structures of their time; their perplexity is not unlike ours today. It seems as though two forces come into conflict in which the harsher overcomes the gentler. Political and economic forces clash with the strength of God's law.

Israel has to become involved in international dealings: it has to get a king like other nations. It has to continue in this direction – otherwise it is lost. The kings, the generals and the top managers of the time had their own views and did not make much of the priestly and prophetic warnings. And at the same time, it was through following this pattern of development that God's people was lost. They saw no prospect of obeying the laws of the Lord and listening to the prophets. Not only did the year of jubilee prove to be a utopian ideal, but the gulf between poor and rich grew wider every day, despite the protests and the clear regulations of the Torah.

Seeking and needing self-sufficiency in a much deeper and more radical sense, they lost themselves. The exile seems to bring Israel's existence to an end. Even though two tribes returned, it did not make very much difference on a social and economic level. What did survive were the regulations of the Torah, the blazing words of the prophets and the frustrating tension between what ought to be done and what could really be done, what actually happened.

Frustration prevailed everywhere. Frustration can quench all initiative and lead to negation. Sometimes, however, such tension can be a stimulus towards a search for new solutions, and discontent with the situation can become the basis for creativity.

From the old covenant to the new

The seeds of this frustration do not lose their hidden force. At the time of the transition from the Old Testament to the New we can see how many people wanted the unity of the covenant to be restored. All kinds of groups were concerned with the old ideals. In the Qumran sect, for example, an attempt was made to realize these ideals in a very radical fashion. You could be accepted into this community only if you gave up your private possessions. It was a community of the poor in which the rich could find a place only if they parted with their riches.

Elements of this 'harsh' interpretation of the intention of the covenant, even affecting material possessions, can be found throughout the New Testament. There are all kinds of different emphases in approach. Its radical spirituality is striking (see below). By the time of Jesus, opposition between poor and rich had increased considerably. The poor sometimes went out on plundering expeditions to provide for their needs. They banded together and waylaid travellers, or robbed the rich in order to be able to keep their heads above water.

In other groups and sects, by contrast, poverty was glorified. A virtue was made of necessity in order to acquire at least some spiritual resources. The contempt for the poor to be found in the writings of some rabbis stands in sharp contrast to this. For them, poverty was worse than sickness, and was avoided like the plague. The 'people of the land', i.e. the country proletariat, were therefore wholeheartedly despised by the rich rabbis.

We have already seen Luke's particular concern for those who are despised. For him, the rich man can indeed be saved, but only if he can give up everything that he has (Luke 14.35). True, the poor is not the only member of the new kingdom, but he is its true heir and has precedence. The reference here is clearly to those who are materially poor, hungry and sorrowful, as they appear in the Sermon on the Mount (Matt. 5.4, 6; Luke 6.21), in short, the socially deprived.

Here, too, the covenant is the basis of concern for the poor. It is reminiscent of the covenant that Jesus can address the poor (Luke) or the poor in spirit (Matthew) and that the whole of the gospel can be described as the gospel of the poor. In any case, to hunger and thirst (Luke) is virtually the same as to hunger and thirst for righteousness (Matthew), because the latter is in fact to hunger and thirst for a specific solution to the problem of poverty. Righteousness here is not what dogmatic theologians call the justification of the godless, but, as H. Ridderbos puts it, the 'royal righteousness' which is described so clearly in Psalm 72.

The interesting thing is that this righteousness is to be found in the context of a deep bond of faith. As we have seen (pp. 41ff.), that was already the case in the Old Testament, but in the New Testament the spiritual factor is very markedly present. As a result, however – and this is the essential point – the material element was emphasized even more strongly, rather than being neglected. For one element to increase does not mean that another element decreases. In our discussions about the horizontal and the vertical, man and God, and so on, we often find that one is stressed at the cost of the other. That never happens in the Bible; on the contrary, the spiritual aspect accentuates the material aspect. That emerges clearly if we compare the differences in approach between the Gospels of Matthew and Luke, for example, in the Beatitudes.

Matthew speaks of the poor in spirit, Luke exclusively of the poor. After the Beatitude about the poor, Luke adds a 'Woe to you', directed towards the rich (Luke 6.24), which is absent from Matthew. 'Blessed are you that hunger now, for you shall be satisfied', says Luke (6.21), and goes on to say by contrast, 'Woe to you that are full now, for you shall hunger.' Matthew says, 'Blessed are those who hunger and thirst for righteousness, for they shall be satisfied' (5.6).

The difference might perhaps be attributed to a problem of translation. As I pointed out, the original Aramaic and Hebrew used different words for the poor, and some of them may have been nearer to poverty in the spiritual sense than others. Also, it may be that in Matthew two beatitudes have been combined: 'Blessed are the poor', and 'Blessed are the people of the spirit'. It is more probable that Matthew and Luke each wrote for a different 'public' and that each has shaped the traditional texts about Jesus for his own particular public. In that case, Matthew clearly has less concern to remind his audience of the materially poor than Luke. His problem is that of people who are caught up in the tradition and lack the spiritual power to break out of it. In his gospel, Matthew tries to introduce his readers to spiritual riches and power, and to restore true religion. Luke has a greater social orientation, and is more concerned with material needs. This difference can also be seen in their approach to the story of the rich young man. In Matthew (19.21), the renunciation of possessions, which is what Jesus ultimately requires, is bound up with wanting to be perfect. He is looking for a completely spiritual life. Luke is much more laconic (18.22), and is concerned with the one thing that this Pharisee still lacks. The Pharisee is told to sell all that he has. For Matthew, that is a prerequisite for a perfect life; for Luke, it is a 'normal' demand. In the story of Lazarus, Luke makes the disproportion between rich and poor a radical one (16.19–31). The rich man cannot be saved. After his death, he will not be taken up into Abraham's bosom, but will be tormented in the underworld. He has already had his reward. And again Luke regards this as the norm. There is no need to warn the rich man's kinsmen: they have been enlightened enough. They have Moses and the prophets (v. 30), who are clear enough on this point.

One might say that Matthew and Luke both begin from the unity of God's ordinances and from the one covenant with all its mutually interconnected demands. Luke stresses this unity above all by drawing attention to actual relationships between poor and rich. The kingdom of God passes by the rich because they are no good. With an eye to the group for which he is writing, Matthew is more concerned with the spiritual character of Christian discipleship and thus arrives at the need for the restoration of the covenant. The poor in spirit are those who live by the same grace as Luke's poor. In principle, the hungry (Luke) and those who hunger after righteousness belong together. These are not contrasting terms, but particularized designations. The evangelists adapt the one concern in Jesus' words to what they feel necessary for their group. By being made specific, the one great truth is translated into the lesser truth relevant to these people in this situation.

Poverty in the New Testament

Not only in Matthew and Luke, but also in all the other parts of the New Testament, the view of poverty is influenced by the coming of Jesus and the promise of his kingdom, as a fulfilment of the Old Testament. The unity of the covenant and its relationships, about which the Old Testament speaks, dreams and prophesies, and on the basis of which it attacks the widening gulf between poor and rich, finds its fulfilment in the dawning of the Messianic age.

However, something quite unexpected happens. In the person of Jesus, the poor man himself appears on the stage. Jesus did not have a roof over his head or a bed to sleep on; there was no place for him to be born in (Luke 2.7), no place where he could lay his head during his lifetime (Matt. 8.20; Luke 9.58), and he ended up in the place of the skull, when all other places on earth were barred to him. His poverty was total and fundamental. Unlike tourists to developing countries, he had no return ticket. He identified himself utterly with mankind. His solidarity was complete. There are even moments in his life when his dependence is so great that he himself cannot go on carrying his own cross. And he dies, naked, on a gibbet. Only his grave is with the rich.

All this gives the gospel an amazing, a unique perspective. In our time, almost all films register poverty from the perspective (the camera standpoint) of the rich. The poor become objects. Westerners go through the slums and shoot harrowing scenes and enlarge the details which interest them. When Kenyan students reversed the roles and in turn began to film the behaviour of European reporters and tourists, they caused deep offence. No one wants to be an object, in other words, an example of suffering. The New Testament constantly adopts the perspective of the poor.

49

The first Christians 'looked on life from the perspective of the outcast, the helpless, the prisoners and the condemned'.[10]

In the famous parable of the good Samaritan, Jesus depicts human life from the gutter. There lies the victim, on the point of death. It is through his eyes that we see the priest and the Levite going past and the Samaritan finally stopping. 'That is how the beggar looks at things, and Jesus the righteous one . . . is himself one of the beggars.' C. W. Mönnich, the author who makes this point, goes on to call faith more a perspective than a conviction.

So throughout the discussion about the rich and the poor, it is important to see who is saying what. It makes all the difference whether 'Blessed are the poor' is said by someone as poor as Jesus, or by a rich man. In the first case it is a beatitude which can bring consolation to the poor. In the second case it can even be a pious pretext through which the rich man safeguards his own privileges, leaving the poor man in his original state while giving himself an aura of sanctity. The same saying can take on very different meanings, depending on the perspective from which it is spoken.

It is also important to remember that the sayings of Jesus are addressed to different audiences. For the poor to be told that they are fortunate because their worth does not depend on their possessions, is no reason for the rich to abandon them to their poverty. This text in Luke is not intended for the rich. They should listen to Matthew ('Blessed are the poor in spirit'); that is quite enough for them (=us) to be getting on with.

The gospel is written from the perspective of the poor man. The basis of the New Testament message is the incarnation: the Word was made flesh. God's solidarity is not just a matter of words, but of deeds. He comes to man in poor, vulnerable, human flesh. He has taken upon himself the form of a slave (Phil. 2.7). He was as lowly as the least of the Christian brotherhood. And it is among them that he can still be found today (Matt. 25.31–36).

So it is no coincidence that in his opening address in Luke's gospel this Messiah announces the acceptable year of the Lord (4.18). The year of jubilee has dawned. The seven characteristics of the Messianic age have been made manifest:

The blind see, the lame walk,
the lepers are cleansed, the deaf hear,
the dead live, the prisoners are released,
and the poor have the gospel preached to them.

We can see from John the Baptist's bitter beatitude (Luke 7.23) how concerned the Messiah is with poverty. When John was in prison, some of his disciples asked whether Jesus really was the Messiah. Jesus gave a strange answer. For the characteristic of the messianic age which was most important for the imprisoned Baptist, the release of prisoners, he substituted the harrowing comment, 'Blessed is he who takes no offence at me.'

Thus the emphasis comes to be placed exclusively on the phrase 'the poor have the gospel preached to them'. Evidently the 'blessedness' of this solidarity was important for John. Furthermore, the Messiah himself was clearly concerned with it. He had to be poor himself. Jesus' answer to John is concerned with the characteristics of the Messiah.

Like the Essenes, to whose order he possibly belonged, John the Baptist adopted the spirituality of the *anawim*, the righteous poor. But the fact that the Messiah himself should be one of the poor was so astonishingly new that all Jewish groups in the time of Jesus inevitably found it offensive.

Jesus' 'vicarious poverty', as Hans-Rüdi Weber calls it,[11] is a deliberate and unprecedented identification with the 'suffering servant' in Deutero-Isaiah, who is often recalled, especially in the gospel of Matthew (Matt. 12.17–21; Isa. 42.1–4; Matt. 8.17; Isa. 53.4). Jesus is the poor man. His hands are empty. He has nothing to give, because he does not own anything. Jesus transforms this scandalous poverty into radical love. Those who have empty hands cannot bestow any charity. They cannot give anything but themselves. From this great change, this representative action on the part of Jesus, the new kingdom is born. And in this way the 'acceptable year of the Lord', the year of jubilee, begins.

The land lies fallow. Its fruits are there for anyone who wants them. So the disciples can leave their bits and pieces behind. They need not be anxious. Debts are remitted, and woe to anyone who claims the year of jubilee only for himself and not for others, like the man in the parable whose debts are remitted by the king and who then goes out and forces his fellow slave to pay up. According to John Howard Yoder,[12] the fifth commandment, 'And forgive us our debts, as we forgive our debtors', is a prayer typical of the year of jubilee.

As he proclaims the dawning of the year of jubilee ('Today this scripture has been fulfilled in your hearing', Luke 4.21), Jesus is extremely critical of anything to do with the establishment, of anyone who is not prepared to let go and remains attached to possessions and power. His own poverty makes this criticism more than mere words, easily spoken: his life is testimony to his solidarity with the poor. This nearness of the kingdom of God, this acceptable year, calls for detachment from every care and for complete trust in God (Matt. 6.25–34; Luke 12.22–32). For this reason, God and mammon cannot go together. God guarantees freedom and liberation, mammon the opposite: possession and being possessed.

As a result, in principle the first choice must be for the kingdom. The rest follows. Jesus was obviously quite indifferent to possessions. He had detached himself from them. Originally he was one of the middle class. His father was a *tekton*, something like a contractor, an architect, a bricklayer, a carpenter, a coach-maker, or a furniture maker. But worldly goods did not seem to mean anything to Jesus. He asked his disciples to break with their families and leave their houses, fields and occupations. They had to learn how to give things away and expect nothing in return (Luke 6.30).

Even Jerome, church father and ascetic (c. AD 400), found this difficult. He said that the commandment was difficult, harsh and contrary to nature. He found a way round it by quoting Matt. 19.12: 'He who is able to receive this, let him receive it.'

However, Jesus was never narrowly moralistic. His indifference to possessions was so great that he allowed himself to be supported by rich women. He had no quarrel with having possessions or money if they were used to support parents (Mark 7.9), or lent without hope of return (Matt. 5.42 and parallel passages). Zacchaeus only gave away half his possessions (Luke 10.8). Jesus was fond of eating and drinking well, and was criticized for it ('a glutton and a drunkard', Matt. 11.19; Luke 7.34). He was certainly not an ascetic, nor was he a member of the Essenes. He ate with the rich and even with those for whom he had no sympathy. Anyone who acts in this way does not view possessions with the critical and fanatical eyes of a radical ascetic.

All kinds of anti-social attitudes are illustrated in the parables of Jesus, but they are usually in the background, and are seldom polemical. Jesus himself uses the classical definition of property: 'Am I not allowed to do what I choose with what belongs to me?' (Matt. 20.15). To this question, any understanding person nowadays has to say no, certainly if he is a Christian. Even liberals do not adopt such an individualistic liberal standpoint today. Apparently Jesus does not propose any new theory about property. His attitude towards it displays the offensive freedom and openness characteristic of his attitude towards the powers of the state, the Roman authorities and their Jewish collaborators.[13]

However, Jesus is extraordinarily vehement where mammon gets people in its grasp, breaks up their relationships and breeds antagonisms. As soon as wealth becomes an obsession and dominates a man's life, we hear the words, 'Woe to you.' Or, in the terms which we have been exploring in this chapter: as soon as the righteousness of the covenant is attacked, Jesus calls an inexorable halt. The way in which he and his disciples abandon the sacred cow of property, family and power is meant to be shocking. This demonstration is certainly not ascetical or naive idealism; I would prefer to call it an almost anarchistic relativism. By that I mean that Jesus is so bound up with God and his ordinances, so devoted to God's law and infected by the joy and freedom which go with bearing witness to God, that he can make light of human ordinances and laws, customs and practices. He criticizes them and makes his own contribution to them. For Jesus and his disciples, this relativism is heightened by a keen expectation for the future. They lived in the sphere of the last things, the *eschata*.[14] This eschatological awareness produced a creative freedom for which it was impossible that human patterns and human structures should ever have the last word.

Paul is in fact our earliest witness to this eschatological awareness. We can see how strong it is for him by the way in which he begins from the resurrection of Christ. The Messiah has come and completed his work. The world is ready for the harvest. This belief leads Paul, too, to make light of property and other ties. The limitations of race, status, religion, sex, slavery and freedom no longer hold now that the Messiah has come (Col. 3.11; Gal. 3.28). His message of grace and justification, reconciliation and freedom, is directly connected with the poverty of Jesus: 'You know the grace of our Lord Jesus Christ, that though he was rich, yet for our sake he became poor, so that by his poverty you might become rich' (II Cor. 8.8). The world of Paul's time was dominated by the contrasts between rich and poor, slave and free, man and woman, Jew and Gentile. That Paul in fact did away with this opposition must have had an uncommonly strong, almost revolutionary effect in the ancient world. His message created an exceptional community of free men, who were so free that they could continue to live even under the old structures. But the pattern of this world was beginning to pass away (I Cor. 7.29ff.).

In his book on Paul, H. Ridderbos speaks in this connection of the 'relative significance of the social position in which one finds himself in view of being a Christian'.[15] This relativistic approach to social circumstances is not prompted by indifference, fanaticism or unworldliness. Far less does it arise because the present no longer counts, given that the new future kingdom is at hand. Precisely because the new kingdom is coming and has come, every man finds a new value in Christ. As a result, Ridderbos points out, 'a renewal of social relationships must become possible and necessary from within'.[16]

Paul must have been aware of the explosive force of the gospel that he presented. In I Cor. 7 he compares being a slave with being circumcised. He had argued that Gentiles who became Christians did not have to be circumcised. This view was vigorously opposed in other Jewish circles. The disagreement became polarized, and there was a good deal of disunity. By approaching slavery in the same open way, Paul must have known that he would produce the same turbulent effect.

Certainly in so bustling a place as Corinth. The 'not many wise, not many powerful, not many of noble birth' (I Cor. 1.26) who had joined the community there had become abundantly rich in Christ (I Cor. 1.5). There were marked differences between the large group of poor people and a small, rich upper class. This last group abused their position not only in Corinthian society but also within the church and even at the Lord's table (I Cor. 11.20). They kept to themselves, feasted on the food they brought with them and at the Lord's Supper neglected the hungry while they got drunk. In so doing, Paul says, they eat judgment upon themselves because they do not discern the body (I Cor. 11.29). The unity of the new community in Christ was denied and disrupted by this behaviour. Its social consequences brought out the basic religious error.

The Hellenistic world set great store by status and reputation. The Gentile Christians had introduced these class distinctions into the church. For them to be told that God had chosen the un-attractive and the despised in order 'to bring to nothing things that are', is more than an echo of Mary's Magnificat (Luke 1). It is difficult to understand this as anything but a subversive act of God. By its very constitution, the community is a threat to the existing order.

Of course it is always difficult to establish what the effect of certain words will have been on their original audience, but words of this kind must have sounded very much like a provocation. I Cor. 1.28, for example, almost sounds like seditious language. The RSV translates it fairly neutrally: God chose 'what is low and despised in the world, even things that are not, to bring to nothing things that are'. The literal meaning is: 'break up the existing state of things'.

The New English Bible uses harsher language: 'He has chosen things low and contemptible, mere nothings, to overthrow the existing order.' The existing order must be destroyed through God's preposterous intervention. This whole passage makes it clear that the existing order which must be overthrown also includes material factors. The parallel with 'things contemptible' leaves no doubt about that.

God's grace is a force which robs existing structures, even political structures, of their power. Paul was anything but a political revolutionary. He sent a runaway slave back to his master Philemon (albeit carrying a letter which regarded Philemon's ownership of him from a similar new perspective and in fact radically put it in question). However, Paul must have been well aware of the implications of his remarks to a community in a city like Corinth, with explosive social tensions which were also having a marked effect within the community. It is the self-same anarchy that we find in the message of Jesus (see note 18 below), but with more of a social focus.

These are not isolated statements. In I Tim. 6.10, the love of money is said to be the root of all evil. And those who read the Letter of James will come up against the sort of passionate comments on society that we found in Paul. Originally, the church to whom James was writing consisted predominantly of poor people. In due course, rich people also joined, claiming a special position in the community by virtue of their possessions and riches. Because of their prominent social position they demanded the best places in the congregation as well. This was a fundamental denial of this new community in Christ (James 2.1–13). James rebukes them for it:

Come now, you rich, weep and howl for the miseries that are coming upon you. Your riches have rotted and your garments are moth-eaten. Your gold and silver have rusted, and their rust will be evidence against you and will eat your flesh like fire. You have laid up treasure for the last days. Behold, the wages of the labourers who mowed your fields, which you kept back by fraud, cry out; and the cries of the harvesters have reached the ears of the Lord of hosts. You have lived on the earth in luxury and in pleasure; you have fattened your hearts in a day of slaughter. You have condemned, you have killed the righteous man; he does not resist you. (James 5.1–6).

A Christian revolution?

Property and riches did not pose problems only to Jews and Christians. The question was under discussion throughout the Graeco-Roman world of the day. 'Possessions are sin' is an expression which occurs in Plato and Josephus, and is repeated long into the early Christian period.

'Those who have God in common, as Father, and do not hold their possessions in common, act sinfully.' Parallels to this patristic comment can be found in texts like Acts 2.44, 'And all who believed were together and had all things in common', and Acts 4.32, 'And no one said that any of the things which he possessed was his own, but they had everything in common.' Being of one heart and soul, as this verse puts it, also has implications for material possessions.

The Bible is not unique in this respect. Similar expressions could well be found in Plato's *Republic*, and the Scythians were known for the way in which they shared possessions.

The comment in I Tim. 6.10, 'The love of money is the root of all evil', might well have been said by Democritus or Diogenes, as Martin Hengel demonstrates with a wealth of quotations.[17] Consequently the earliest church in Jerusalem has been explained in terms of ancient Greek ideals, and there has been talk of a communism of love or a patriarchate of love (Ernst Troeltsch). However, we need to be careful here. This approach misses the deepest reason for the Bible's concern with social questions. We have already described how Old Testament preaching and tradition prompts thought and action on the basis of the unity of the covenant and calls attention to the demands of righteousness within the covenant.

In the New Testament, this line was developed further and included within the perspective of God's new kingdom announced and inaugurated in Christ. This kingdom is all-embracing. It asks for and gives – or rather, it gives and asks for – a new form of existence in which the last things (the ultimate future) become today's norm. This eschatological prospect is concerned with an unprecedented certainty which teaches us to let go and sit lightly to things because we are assured of God's love. In this way it unmasks the pseudo-certainties of our existence by means of a freedom which is deeply rooted, because it is founded on love. Acts 2.42–47; 4.32–37 show a church which came into being through faith in this freedom and began to hold all its possessions communally, almost as a matter of course. Everything was shared; personal property no longer existed. People lived exclusively in the light of the new kingdom which had already dawned in their community and which before long would spread throughout the world. Their community was an advance outpost of the kingdom on earth, a new creation, a fore-runner of God's order, 'a kind of first fruits of God's creatures' (James 1.18).

No rules were laid down to enforce the sharing of possessions, as happened in the Qumran sect, which was active at the same time in the wilderness of Judah. Qumran might be described as a Jewish pattern of poverty which had hardened into legalism.

The difference between the Christians and Qumran is the element of free choice. In Christ's community there is no need to give up possessions. No one is forced to, as is clear from the story of Ananias and Sapphira (Acts 5.1–11). This particular couple pretended to hand over all their possessions to the community, but sought security for themselves by keeping something back. The problem was not what they kept back (they could do what they wanted with their possessions, Acts 5.4); it was their deceitfulness. We can see what importance was attached to this sort of incident in the community. Surreptitious withholding of possessions, pseudo-dedication, was regarded as a lie against the Holy Spirit.

The basis of this community in the literal sense is the attractive-ness of the freedom shown by Jesus. The resurrection had under-lined this freedom and was proof of the trustworthiness of Jesus and his ministry. The Spirit given at Pentecost furthered such a life-style and helped to spread it beyond the boundaries of Israel. In contrast to the Christian community in Jerusalem, the Qumran sect sought to accumulate possessions. The group itself was rich and increased its wealth by compelling new members to donate their private property to the group. We can see this as an attempt to accumulate corporate possessions. If a new member gave false information about his possessions, he was put in solitary confinement for a year and his food rations were reduced by a quarter. The community described in Acts was a voluntary association inspired by the freedom of the risen Lord, with a minimum of organization and a maximum of expectations. True, the community could not exist like this for long. Organizational structures had to be developed. Arrangements were made for the care of widows, and a diaconate was instituted. Overseers and elders found a place alongside the apostles. As a result of the famine which occurred in the 40s, during the reign of Claudius, Jerusalem itself became dependent on collections from the churches abroad.

However, what happened within this new sect of people who later came to be called Christians was not just a flash in the pan and amounts to more than an ethical or religious revival. It was a realization of some aspects of the kingdom of God, a total revolution which also affected attitudes towards possessions. Many people have attempted to describe the revolution in rather more detail. All kinds of terms have been used, many of them borrowed from Marxism. Finally, in Communism, it inspired an attempt to regulate the whole of society, beginning with the control of the means of production. However, the danger here is that biblical phenomena are explained by means of terms and thought-patterns which arose at a much later time (in the case of Marxism and Leninism within the last two centuries). There is more than a theoretical risk that such an approach will force the Bible into an alien pattern and will make it mean whatever the interpreter wants. However, that is the risk in any translation. In the last resort, any terms we employ now are coloured by our own circumstances. When they are used in connection with the past, there is every chance of their being misunderstood.

The biblical record makes it quite clear that salvation is always bound up with possessions and society. The kingdom of God affects all our lives. The intervention of God and his Messiah brings about a shift in the balance of power. Our world is no longer controlled by self-interest, covetousness, sin, or the profit motive, but by the gentle powers of a crucified Lord who has been raised from the dead. His rule embraces the whole earth, and calls for a completely new life-style.

This is not a revolt of the kind in which Zealots were involved. To use Belo's terms,[18] their revolt was a utopian movement with Messianic expectations and really sought to restore earlier methods of production. A revolt is not concerned with renewal, but with restoration of the old order. It is reform with an eye to restoration.

M. de Jonge also points to the difference between Jesus and the Zealots.[19] This can be seen above all in the significance of the cross. To put it bluntly, a Zealot is prepared to crucify others for his own great ideal, but will not let himself be crucified unless it is forced on him. Anyone who, like Jesus, does not resist but allows himself to be crucified, cannot be the leader of a revolt. 'The cross is the radical negation of all zealotism.' Belo rightly points out that Christianity is concerned with a renewal of the whole of life and the world.

The messianic reality and the life-style that goes with it are all-embracing, and affect every level of human existence and society. In this sense we can clearly speak of a total revolution. All life is affected by the reality of the new kingdom, including the means of production, political forces and ideological categories. However, as Belo himself has to concede, this is achieved in a non-revolutionary way. Nor does it come about through the accumulation of power or through a historical process of increasing conflict. According to Belo, the strategy of Christianity is non-revolutionary and radically communistic (in contrast to the kind of bourgeois strategy typified by the Russian revolution). Rostagno uses vaguer terms and talks of a kind of social revolution.

At the same time, both commentators make it clear that in the ministry of Jesus and the coming of his kingdom a revolutionary development takes place which affects all relationships and all phenomena. We can see from Paul's appearance in Corinth (see pp. 54ff.) above) that God is emphatically concerned with the relationship between social classes. He chooses the weak groups, the lower class, to demolish the unjust and oppressive structures of this world.

Though the gospel does not favour the poor, as though they were *ipso facto* better than the rich, it is in fact the gospel of the poor. Those who have nothing to lose find it easiest to understand the gospel of free grace. Their place at the heart of Christ's community is the proof of God's new order. It is no accident that the weak and the poor are thus chosen. Their role is not an extra to the gospel, nor are they the touchstone of the community. Their membership of the community, tangible and concrete, is itself the truth. Here is the Messiah. God is in their midst in his true character – as the God who chooses the poor. The rich are welcome, but on the same conditions as the poor: they too must live only by grace.

So there is more here than a patriarchate of love, a community with optimal provisions for all members. The church is not a charitable society of people who have a certain amount to spare for others. It is a community of people who are always holding out their hands. Each one lives from the love given through Christ. Grace is not a minor matter; it is the foundation of the community. So by definition the church cannot ignore social structures. Its very existence is contrary to the existing order and thus a source of inspiration to anyone looking for real renewal, and a source of scandal to anyone concerned to continue the old pattern.

A decision for or against the community of Christ raises the penetrating question whether we are in fact prepared to live wholly and utterly by God's grace. So it is unthinkable that people who champion *sola gratia*, grace alone, in theology should allow the pattern of society under which they live to be dominated by the existing order, which tends to be governed by its own interests rather than by grace.

The converse is also true. However much the Bible may be

interested in material concerns, these concerns are always viewed from the new perspective of a kingdom which has arrived and will manifest itself before very long.

In that case, violent change is hardly necessary. It is clearly of secondary importance. What predominates is the almost presumptuous attitude that injustice is *ipso facto* a thing of the past. It is an anachronism and does not fit into Christ's new time. Riches corrupt, and the pattern of this world is steadily passing away. Anyone who nevertheless insists on working to the old pattern of possessions and power and riches has a pretty poor understanding. He knows nothing at all about grace.

The Bible is aware of the pain and hardship which opposition to the new life-style will bring. A book like Revelation is written in the confident expectation that the new Jerusalem is on the way: Babylon (=the power of the Roman empire) is fallen. What remain are the convulsions of a lost kingdom which cannot stand up to the kingdom of the Messiah. The beast yields to the lamb.

In this sense we can certainly talk of a revolution, but provided that the term is not misunderstood, we should call it an anarchistic revolution. The victory of the Kyrios, the new Lord, has destroyed the power of all the rulers of this world (I Cor. 2.6). He will dethrone all lordship and strength and power (I Cor. 15.24).

This 'anarchistic revolution' is not based on the caprice of individuals, the corporate interest of the state, the compelling majority of half plus one. It is based on the irresistible victory of the Lord. It is sanctified anarchy (see also p. 51 above). It is freedom bound up with Jesus. This fundamental freedom is one of the factors which attacked the iron unity of the Roman empire from within, as in Nebuchadnezzar's dream (Dan. 2.1–49). A stone cut by no human hand rolls down towards a statue made of iron, clay, bronze, silver and gold, the symbols of the kingdoms of this earth, and shatters it completely. For the God of heaven, Daniel says, 'will set up a kingdom which shall never be destroyed ... It shall break in pieces all these kingdoms and bring them to an end ... and it shall stand for ever ...'(Dan. 2.44).

The small, vulnerable community of the time was like that

stone. Its God-given freedom enabled it to withstand all kinds of pressures and persecutions. An open community developed which had no concern about status, high or low. People lived by one another's resources and paid no attention to worldly distinctions.

With its power, its faith and its demonstrable solidarity the community, seen as a forerunner and a model of the new creation (James 1.18), needed no force to achieve its goal. But it did not last long. The church very quickly became bourgeois. We can already find tendencies in this direction in the Pastoral Epistles (Timothy, Titus). This development was most regrettable. Of course, one might argue that it made the church more accessible, and prevented it from being swallowed up in history as one more sect. At the same time, though, some essential characteristics were lost. Without doubt, these included freedom towards possessions and income. The echoes of this economic renewal and a solidarity which even extended to the sharing of possessions continued to resound for a long time both inside and outside the church. In fact they have never completely died down. The Roman empire collapsed. The power of wealth and economic forces has proved more tenacious. The gospels and epistles give much more frequent warnings about the danger of riches than about the Roman authorities, and do so with good reason. Kingdoms pass away, but our materialistic attitude tends to persist.

On that note both Old and New Testaments end. The Old Testament prophets did not really succeed in achieving renewal in the economic sphere. A beginning has been made through the appearance of Jesus and a community which lives in his strength, but here too, stagnation is a constant threat. However, the challenge remains, and freedom retains its attractiveness. Further-more, we have seen what is possible. There has been a man who was able to live without the security of power and possessions. His followers could do the same thing. A community of very ordinary people demonstrated not only that all this was possible, but that it was pleasant, a source of joy, a life of freedom.

Righteousness is the word which sums up this protest against the widening of the gulf between poor and rich. It relates to the structures which produce poverty and riches. It is a far-reaching term. At the same time, however, it points towards freedom. Moralism, compulsion, spiritual control, a law which kills, all these run counter to the biblical concept of righteousness. The law of God's righteousness may be a law with its own authority, but it does not exert compulsion, at least not in the New Testament. How could the writers of the New Testament ever imagine that one day Christians would be in the majority and would be able to choose their emperors and their presidents, becoming powerful enough to order society in accordance with their particular view? The New Testament community was not prepared for that. The claims made by the first Christians were great, but their position was that of a tiny minority. Their politics inevitably had to be those of a minority group. All they could do was to be a creative example.

After Constantine (AD 313), Christianity was in a position to exercise power over a long period. Its record in this respect is not very impressive, certainly not when it comes to regulations about possessions and power. Only on the periphery of the church, in monasteries, in heretical groups and in sects, did something of the old ideal remain alive. Now that the Constantinian dream is almost at an end and the church in Europe longs for its return, the question of a model again becomes urgent. Might the Christian community succeed once again in discovering its freedom and in opening up the sources of its creativity? Surely now is the time.

Throughout this chapter we have been concerned with the rediscovery of the unity of the covenant on which the Old Testament lays so much stress and which is grounded in the reality of the Messiah and his kingdom that exists and is yet to come. At the Assembly of the World Council of Churches in Nairobi in 1976, Bishop Mortimer Arias rightly pleaded for a 'holistic approach', that it is to say, an approach which takes into account all God's promises and demands. It is worth remembering, though, that this unity in the Bible is in fact an artificial one. Even in a book like this, it is necessary to look for the unity in the multiplicity of facts which sometimes seem to conflict. I have already discussed the differences in the treatment of poverty in the gospels of Matthew and Luke, or those between the wisdom literature and the prophets. Paul's 'theology' of consistent grace and the attractive, profound freedom of Jesus' own faith are the components which make this unity visible. However, it is dangerous to lay too much stress on this unity or even to be over-hasty in interpreting the different contrasts of which it is built up as supplementary features. The Bible is indeed a connected whole. But the nature of the material requires us sometimes to stress one aspect at the expense of another. The one truth manifests itself one-sidedly in the aspect which is relevant at a particular moment.

Riches are a curse and a blessing. Both aspects are true. But that does not mean that they are interchangeable within the unity of the covenant. Rich oppressors cannot resort to the argument that Abraham, after all, was a rich man. For anyone who acquires his riches through deceit and uses them to oppress the poor, riches are plainly a curse. Such use of riches is the target of Luke's lament. That is why it is so important in our quotation of biblical material not only to take historical and archaeological facts into account, but also to remember social and political conditions, along with the distribution of means of production. Only when we have taken all these aspects into account can we realize the significance of the prophetic protest (which is also a political protest), the beatitudes or any judgment on the rich, and try to apply them to our world.

When we take the political and social background into account, and understand the structures within which men live out their lives, we can see the force of a biblical text. Here one-sidedness comes into its own.

We do not need a sophisticated approach in which ultimately the truth can be anything and in fact means nothing. The one truth is specific and therefore one-sided by definition. Too often the poor are put off with pious texts, and their exploiters give themselves an aura of respectability by means of biblical quotations. The harshness, the social and structural connotations of the word 'righteousness', are a powerful antidote to any misuse of this kind.

5

Poverty and the People of God: Solidarity

Righteousness is an all-embracing concept. It is concerned with the whole of the covenant, the totality of relationships between God and man and animals and things. To reduce it to material circumstances, to the relationship between poor and rich, can even lead to one-sidedness. We may be right to be one-sided, but at the same time we must realize that the Bible does not consider poverty only in terms of structures. It also sees poverty in terms of mutual solidarity. Poverty is not just a matter of politics; it is just as much an attack on the unity of the people of God. It is intolerable for the community that one person's status should be totally different from that of another. In those circumstances, how it is possible to talk of one another as brothers and sisters?

We often discover that from family life. When one member of the family enjoys a higher standard of living as the result of a 'better' career, a 'better' marriage, the social differences can ultimately undermine the original cohesion of the family. In the Bible, the covenant extends this cohesion to the whole community as the people of God.

The community as the basis of solidarity

The Old Testament communicates a strong sense of solidarity. The rich who cause poverty through oppression and exploitation will find the Bible diametrically opposed to them (as we saw in the previous chapter). However, there were other reasons for poverty, factors which at that time were certainly outside the sphere of human influence. There were droughts, floods and other natural disasters. There were sickness and death, bringing in their wake widows and orphans who had to get by with no means of support. Man is helpless when confronted with the forces of nature. One would expect the Bible to pay a good deal of attention to the dominant power of fate. Even in modern times, with the technology at our disposal, natural disasters like floods and earthquakes are often seen primarily as acts of God.

It is worth noting that while the caprices of fate play their part in the Bible, they are never stressed. The main problem is not that a father, a husband, is dead, or that no rain falls. The concern of the Bible is always with those who suffer from fate and find no helper. Of course life is hard. And the Bible does not go in for theoretical discussions or explanations as to why one person is more fortunate than another. It stresses, rather, that in face of the caprices of fate, the community ought to be concerned about and care for the victims, accepting them and compensating them for what the forces of nature have destroyed. The community itself is a covenant community of God and man, an antidote against the vicissitudes of fate. Social life is in any case characterized above all by a strong sense of solidarity; the sense of being one people, even the people of God, strengthens this solidarity.

Where there is no solidarity, Israel loses its *raison d'être* as God's people. The law and the prophets find it intolerable that in the promised land itself, among the people of God, some men pride themselves above their fellows and exclude others from the prosperity of a land 'flowing with milk and honey'. There is to be no poverty in this land. 'But there will be no poor among you, for the Lord will bless you in the land' (Deut. 15.4). The fact that nevertheless there are poor, and that they are abandoned to their poverty, is proof that the people of God have ceased to be the people of God. Outside the book of Deuteronomy, this idea is stressed very strongly in the writings of Ezekiel.

'The people of the land have practised extortion and committed robbery; they have oppressed the poor and needy, and have

67

extorted from the sojourner without redress. And I sought for a man among them who should build up the wall and stand in the breach before me for the land, that I should not destroy it, but I found none. Therefore I have poured out my indignation upon them' (Ezek. 22.29–31).

God's people forfeits its rights to existence when there is no longer anyone to champion the poor. The expression 'and there shall be no poor in the land' (Deut. 15.3–11, cf. Matt. 26.11 and parallel passages) is not, as has been suggested more than once, an expression of fatalism. It is not as though poverty were a kind of natural phenomenon, about which nothing could be done. On the contrary, mutual concern is never allowed to be the exception: it is regarded as the normal pattern of life. In that case the question arises whether we should appeal to the Bible in connection with our acts of charity, great or small. To do so makes mutual care an exception, a point at which people are urged with a great deal of trumpeting to depart from their manifestly merciless rules and for once in a while to do good to one another.

Within the biblical community such mutual care is taken for granted. It has to be practised among the brotherhood. 'You shall open wide your hand to your brother, to the needy and to the poor, in the land' (Deut. 15.11). That is quite simply their right. Mutual concern is the rule and not the exception. This brotherhood is the basis for Israel's strength among the nations (Deut. 15.6). Israel is not to thrive on outward displays of power, armaments and the like, but on its inner solidarity. Its power is founded on mutual service. I have already argued that solidarity was the characteristic of the semi-nomadic community. This was especially true of the exodus community. 'This whole people, born as it was from a revolutionary freedom movement in the exodus from Egypt, forged in the trials in the wilderness and brought together by the God of the covenant promises, was summoned to take part in the mighty acts of Yahweh,' says Gélin.[1] To take part in these mighty acts is also to share their benefits.

Sharing the Lord's benefits is a characteristic of the covenant. Possessions and property must also be looked after, assessed and distributed in such a way that every member of the community has his fair share. One man's prosperity is closely connected with that of others. You cannot be rich by yourself. To accept poverty and injustice for larger and smaller groups, or for individuals within the community, would be to regress into the slavery of Egypt. The exodus and its subsequent ratification in the giving of the Law on Sinai brings liberation because in these events God gives all his people freedom from every internal and external constraint. Not only was Israel freed from external dependence, and from foreign 'colonization'; it was also freed from that internal colonization in which one brother exploits another. The prophets keep going back again and again to these inward and outward signs of the exodus as a norm for the structure of Israelite society. The people set out towards their destiny as a new brotherhood. Behind this ideal of brotherhood is a deep sense that every man is created by God and part of the divine purpose. Faith in God as creator leads to respect for the other person as a worthwhile individual, even outside the bounds of tribe, family and people. Faith in God as Creator is thus more than a familiar, formal belief. It has direct consequences for our behaviour towards one another. This is illustrated by a famous rabbinic story.

The Hasidic rabbi Levi Isaac of Berdichev, 'the merciful one', who later became legendary, was already well-known for his wisdom and his insight when he was young. From far and near people came to ask his advice. He was still living with his father-in-law. One day he remarked that he was going back to his teacher again. His father-in-law was very cross, thought it unnecessary and was angry at the drop in domestic income. However, the rabbi had his way, and went off for six months. When he got back, his father-in-law asked him bitterly, 'What did you learn?' 'That there is one creator of heaven and earth.' The father-in-law now got very cross indeed. 'Even my servant, Ivan the Russian, knows that.' And so he did. When Ivan the Russian was called, he replied, 'Yes master, I know it, the whole world knows it, the whole world says it.' The rabbi commented: 'That is just it – the whole world knows it, the whole world says it, but have they learnt it?' Anyone who has really learnt that God is creator deals differently with God's creatures and his creation.

This knowledge that God is the creator affects not only relationships among God's people but also their relationships outside. This is clear from Israel's special concern for foreigners. Man, any man, is in the image of his creator. Any infringement of human rights is an infringement of God's purposes and thus an infringement of God himself. The society God wants is a society based on the equality of man. Inequality is a violation of God's will. When that develops among his people, they forfeit their vocation and their right to exist.

The history of Israel and the history of the church are often the history of the forfeiture of this vocation. The official church tends to lose faith in this biblical ordinance, leaving it to be put into practice in sects and groups. In biblical times there were the Rechabites, the Qumran sect and later the Ebionites. Whatever else they may have been, these groups were in any event attempts to realize the ideal of brotherhood.

A new brotherhood

The New Testament is a powerful stimulus to this ideal. The founder of Christianity was himself poor. His identification with others was unprecedented. He gave himself up for the new community. The church is built on his self-surrender. He can be criticized in almost every respect, for his origin, his status, his pretensions, but one thing is irrefutable: his solidarity. Jesus is the embodiment of the poor man. He does not attempt to disown this image. He does not look for ways of being reconciled with the state. Ambition and greed are alien to him. From the beginning, the community founded by him and rooted in him was characterized by a very practical solidarity. That is why it found universal favour. The members of the community did not address one another by formal titles, and were unconcerned with social status symbols. They did not call one another 'Your honour', 'Your grace', boss, slave, man or woman: they simply called one another 'brother'.

70

I ought to make it quite clear that this masculine word also included women. It is a pity that our versions obscure the point. It would be better if they could translate *adelphoi* as 'brothers-and-sisters', or substitute a word like 'kinsfolk'. The word 'adelphoi' occurs no less than 30 times in Acts and 130 in Paul. It demonstrates the spiritual affinity of the community. Here the Christian community has taken over the religious title of the people of Israel.

Differences in rank, the categories of a competitive world and social conflicts no longer matter in personal relationships. The important thing is that everyone belongs to the one community of Christ. This community is not just a spiritual community; it is also a community in a material sense. People had everything in common. Their solidarity can be seen from all kinds of mutual concerns: the sharing of goods, the founding of a diaconate, care for widows and involving them in community service (as a special kind of ministry?), and so on (see I Tim. 5.3–16).

Communion at the Lord's table is the centre of this mutual fellowship. It is there that reconciliation takes place, dividing walls collapse and people meet one another in the Lord. The approach from a different perspective does away with tensions which once kept people apart. The quality of the community is determined, not by social standards, but by sharing life together in the grace of the Lord. By definition the community is a community of the poor, those who live from the riches of the Lord who was himself poor. 'For you know the grace of our Lord Jesus Christ, that though he was rich, yet for your sake he became poor, so that by his poverty you might become rich' (II Cor. 8.9). This perspective makes the riches of the rich superfluous. Indeed their riches often prove to be a danger (as is shown, not only by Luke, but also by I Tim. 6.9f.). Riches are a snare, a temptation, which can bring men down in ruin and catastrophe. They cause people a good deal of pain. Provided that we have a roof over our heads and enough to support us, that should be enough. From this spiritual perspective, riches are held to be a danger. They add nothing to the Lord's fellowship. So faith makes the quest for riches unimportant.

71

Anyone who lives in the power of this Lord no longer depends on his possessions and can therefore put what he has at the disposal of the community, with gladness and joy. In this way, the wealth of the rich is purged and transformed into mutual help and support. The poverty of the poor is transformed in the same way. Poverty is not a negative factor in the kingdom of God. No one is any the less as a result of it. Consequently, within the community poverty is transformed and abolished. People learn to share.

Even when the urge to share possessions began to wane, as we can already see from the later letters of Paul, this mutuality was still affirmed strongly.

In the second century, the 'Teaching of the Twelve Apostles', the so-called Didache, can still say, 'Do not turn away the needy, but share everything with your brother, and do not say that it is your own. For if you have what is eternal in common, how much more should you have what is transient' (Didache IV 8). Tertullian (born about AD 160) says: 'All things are common among us but our wives.'[2]

Sharing as a sign of freedom

As we have said, Jesus himself gave up all possessions. He came from a middle-class background. According to Justin Martyr, who lived in the second half of the second century AD, he made yokes and ploughs. At the time of the emperor Domitian (AD 81–96), two of his nephews seem to have owned a small estate with a taxable value of 9000 denarii (one denarius is the wage for a day's work). Paul, too, had no possessions. He lived on what he could earn as a tent-maker, and sometimes on the gifts of others. He belonged at the top of the lowest class. His manual worker's hand was only up to writing in large letters, as he remarks jokingly in Gal. 6.11.

However, neither Jesus nor Paul belong to the proletariat. They did not come from among the poorest of the poor, who are often the centre of so much attention, in theory if not in practice, in the context of present-day development studies.

By their personal example, both Jesus and Paul demonstrated

that people from different backgrounds can come together to form a community. They continued to belong to a particular class, as we can see even from the way in which they talk. But their commitment to sharing with others led to the formation of a community of people which did away with the damnable divisions between people and classes. This came about through a practical demonstration that these divisions were irrelevant, so they could really be broken down and forgotten. Reconciliation was a change of reality. At least to begin with, the community itself largely consisted of the poor and the very poor: 'not many wise according to worldly standards, not many powerful, not many of noble birth' (I Cor. 1.26). Very soon, and certainly by the second half of the second century, rich people also joined. These Christians were predominantly middle-class, but they were also drawn from the circles of the 'god-fearers', who had been attracted by the Jewish mission. Many upper-class women also became Christians. In the church, they found the freedom which was denied them in their own culture. Even the nephew of the emperor Domitian, Flavius Clemens, and his wife Domitilla, seem to have been converts.

We have already seen the reaction of the letter of James to this development, and its fierce attack on these rich people when they demanded special treatment within the community on the basis of their social position outside it, completely disregarding the poor. James is shocked by this further discrimination against the poor. It is scandalous, blasphemy of the good name which has been called over them (James 2.7). He feels as strongly as that. His words conjure up the wrath of the Old Testament prophets. James will not allow this sign of God's purposes to be frustrated again. Anyone who violates God's community violates the name of God. He swears like a trooper.

However, the rich are never rejected. From the beginning, people of 'higher rank' joined the church. We hear of Erastus, the city treasurer (Rom. 16.23); Crispus, president of the synagogue (Acts 18.8); Stephanas and his house (I Cor. 1.16; 16.15, 17); Prisca, Aquila and Philemon, and so on, but to begin with these are exceptions.

73

Moreover, at first the church was confined to the cities. In Israel it also spread to the countryside, but outside Palestine, congregations were concentrated in the cities. The country population, consisting of exploited tenants, poor farmers and agricultural workers, had a harder time than the city proletariat. At a later period, when country people also began to join the church, Pliny anxiously wrote to the emperor Trajan: 'For many of all ages and of every rank, and also of both sexes, are brought into present and future danger by this unbelief.'

All this suggests that the mutual solidarity of Christ's community began to exercise a powerful influence on social structures. People have often been surprised that there are so few direct references in the epistles, or elsewhere in the New Testament, to public witness and proclamation. This is because the community was itself living proof that the grace of God had appeared, bringing salvation to all men, as Paul says to Titus (Titus 2.11). It was clear that society did not have to be ruled by force or by exploitation. The community proved otherwise. It represented an alternative, a new life-style. Love, togetherness, brotherhood still seemed possible. Although Paul does not call for the abolition of class distinctions (or even for the abolition of slavery), he does seek urgently a brotherly love which requires equality (II Cor. 8.14f.). He refers back to the Old Testament: 'He that gathered much had nothing over, and he that gathered little had no lack' (Ex. 16.18). He does not see anything special in this equality: it is a matter of plain justice. What is superfluous for one person supplies the daily needs of another. He uses the same argument over the collection for Jerusalem in the new churches.[3]

The principle of equality was strongly stressed in Greek democracy. Greek law and the Greek form of the city were based on freedom and equality. Equality is also the supreme virtue. So the length and breadth and height of the new Jerusalem are all equal (Rev. 21.10), as was the case with the 'holy of holies' in the old Temple, which in turn derived its form from ancient Egypt. In the New Testament, this ideal of equality and this principle of justice were given a new dimension by the love of Christ and the

74

grace of God. This sovereign grace, which takes no heed of persons (Acts 11.17: 'in a completely equal way', and Matt. 20.12: the irritating parable of the workers in the vineyard, who receive equal wages regardless of the work they have done), looks for equality in externals on the basis of inner need. The coming of the kingdom of God shows that such equality is the fulfilment of earthly aspirations. The tension between eschatological equality (i.e. equality directed towards God's future) and any equality that exists in the present is a stimulus to overcome present tensions, rather than a consolation or an excuse. However, it has already been realized in the community, which is the provisional sphere of God's future.

6

Poverty and the Poor Man's Self-reliance: Spirituality

In the two challenges to poverty and the humiliation of the poor which we have considered so far, the initiative in fact lies with the rich man. He has to show righteousness. He has to teach solidarity. Righteousness and solidarity are the words with which the Bible calls the rich man to order. The poor man is dependent on the rich man's righteousness. The powerful are the ones who are required to show righteousness and to consider the rights of the poor. The poor have been deprived of their rights. The rich will have to restore them.

When it comes to solidarity, the poor man is already at an advantage. In principle, he is of equal worth. There are no distinctions within the community. However, this solidarity is not his problem. He can be sure of that. He has been denied solidarity by society, so once again it is the rich who have to take the initiative. The poor man cannot contribute anything but himself. However, this does not seem to be enough. We have already seen that one of the most wretched aspects of poverty is the contempt which the poor man has to endure. Because he is poor, he is also inferior, second-rate. He no longer counts. Poverty is like a disease. It stigmatizes and humiliates. The poor man has to fall back on himself, and at the same time he becomes reserved. He begins to doubt his own capacity. Perhaps he is inferior; perhaps there is nothing he can do about his inferiority. He no longer believes in change. I had first-hand experience of this in the south of Chile. It was when Salvador Allende was still in power.

Development workers and missionaries had become really optimistic. Land reforms were being carried out, and although the harvests were small, many people found that things were getting better. In the district of Osorno, a large area of land threatened by erosion had been planted with trees at government expense. However, one night local campesinos dug up the trees and destroyed them. They were asked why. They replied, 'When the trees have grown and the land is restored, our harvests will be taken away again.' We could not believe them, and found their attitude discouraging and fatalistic. Six months later, Allende was assassinated and the old oppressive regime was restored.

The poor man's needs

To be able to believe in change, people have to believe that it is possible and that they can achieve it. Living under constant pressure and in desparate circumstances kills hope and quenches the flame of self-reliance. And unless the poor man has self-reliance, any improvement in his condition has to be left to others; it has to come from outside and does not involve the poor man himself.

The poor man should not be primarily an object of concern. Many passages in the Bible insist that the rich need to be concerned about themselves, for example about the soul that they are in danger of losing.

The very words 'justice' and 'solidarity' are not part of the vocabulary of charity; their presupposition is that all men are equal. Here the poor man's own self-reliance is one of the most important factors. He needs to be rescued from his feelings of separateness, inferiority and self-contempt. The Bible is well aware of this. It will have nothing to do with the view that the poor man is not only unfortunate but also inferior. First of all, it affirms that in any case the poor man is not dependent on others in one respect. He has a saviour: the Lord God. There is someone at his side. In his fight against his enemies he can always turn to God and to the house of God: the sanctuary and the Temple. He knows that he will always find a hearing with God. This is especially clear from the psalms. The so-called individual and corporate psalms of lament, like Psalms 3, 5, 6 etc. (laments of the individual) and Psalms 44, 74, 79, 83 etc. (laments of the people) are all set in the sanctuary.

The poor man turns to God. All these psalms of lament follow a characteristic, stereotyped pattern. They form a kind of liturgy: invocation of God, petitions and desires, and then a plea to God and an expression of trust in him. God is the poor man's guarantor, his refuge and his helper. It is God who resists the workers of unrighteousness, the 'evil men', or the 'men of the lie', whoever they may be, and helps the poor man to secure his rights. Whereas other helpers fail, because they are unwilling or incapable, God can always be trusted.

As we saw earlier, this perspective on poverty gives it almost a religious character. It takes on an aura of sanctity. The poor man acquires a halo. One can see, smell, hear that God is with him. Poverty becomes a special quality. The poor man is tranquil (where God is concerned), meek, lowly, humble, completely open and expectant. He has surrendered himself wholly to God. Above all, he is gentle and lowly in heart. Those are the specific characteristics of the poor. Jesus, too, applies them to himself in a well-known saying: 'Come to me, all who labour and are heavy-laden, and I will give you rest. Take my yoke upon you, and learn from me; for I am gentle and lowly in heart' (Matt. 11.28f.). This characteristic attitude of the poor man, his gentleness and lowliness, give poverty a character all of its own. One step further, and poverty itself becomes the basis for salvation. Poverty is ennobled. 'I love poverty. It is God's gift to man. A treasure. And not costly, either,' remarked Rabbi Nahum of Czernobel. He was very poor.

Without this tone of disparagement, such a remark would be extremely dangerous, especially if it were made by a rich man. Gélin's book, which I have already mentioned several times, does not entirely avoid this danger. Gélin feels that an evangelist like Matthew (blessed are the poor in spirit) comes closer to the perfection of the gospel than Luke (blessed are you poor), who pays too much attention to its material aspect. However, the poor receive the promise of salvation, not because they are so poor, but because the all-embracing character of the covenant can be seen so clearly in them.

They are the true people of God when seen from the perspective of the covenant, but not otherwise. Unless we recognize this, there is a risk that poverty might become an end in itself, a holy state which the rich and powerful would do best to tolerate. However, the fact that in the Bible poverty has acquired religious and ethical connotations does not make poverty within society any less a problem; it just places it within the confines of the covenant. Within this covenant, poverty is done away with. Not, however, by making the poor rich. What would be the advantage of that? What is gained if the abolition of poverty simply means that the oppressed now become the oppressors? There is no advantage if a revolution simply reverses roles, rather than putting an end to this social role play. Dictatorship even by the proletariat remains dictatorship. Change does not necessarily lead to improvement. The Bible looks for a different way. Poverty has a positive spiritual component and riches have a negative one. The gospel is intended for both rich and poor.

The helplessness of the rich

Spiritual problems underlie all social and economic problems. Covetousness and the desire for more possessions are shown up in the Bible as mistrust. It is not only remarkable, but disquieting that I Tim. 6.10 calls the love of money the root of all evil. Those who are covetous live on a very narrow basis. They have to have so much because they themselves feel so small. They need something else, other people's possessions, sex, power, because they are so obviously insignificant. In their attempt to escape themselves and God they sap the strength of others as they try to achieve some status. People get so attached to possessions and power because their trust in God and in themselves is so infinitesimally

79

weak. But to put it in old-fashioned terms, anyone who really has been given everything needful for body and soul, for time and eternity, no longer requires other people in order to become himself.

The gospel breaks down this fundamental self-doubt by proclaiming a God who is love, who forgives and reconciles, a liberating God. This liberation begins with man's heart. He is freed. He can be himself. He does not have to become something first. He is already a beloved child of God. This is the seed from which his freedom grows. He can let go because he is held fast.

This basic idea can be found throughout the Bible. For example, it is very prominent in the fourth commandment. Man may (must) rest from his hard labour on the seventh day because the earth and its fullness is already in the good hands of the creator and remains there (Ex. 20.10). In Deuteronomy (5.12–15), the foundation for this trust is the rescue of the Israelites from Egypt at God's hand.

Almost by definition, this applies particularly to the poor. Their whole mode of existence is one of dependence, because there is nowhere for them to turn other than to God. They have to find a foundation for personal self-reliance in their reliance on God. Trust in God gives them an opportunity to express themselves and formulate their complaints. To be able to complain like this is a first step on the way towards liberation.

Dorothee Sölle has some particularly important things to say about suffering and language.[1] She also considers the psalms. Suffering, she comments, makes people dumb. When that happens, they no longer have any defence against utter annihilation. She gives as an example people in German concentration camps whose suffering reduced them to a twilight state; they were so dulled and acquiescent that they even allowed their food to be taken away from them. People called them 'Moslems'. Fate had them completely in its grasp. They had no defences.

Such suffering blunts a person, and when it turns into refusal to accept any help, the result is that a neurosis develops which expresses itself in dull acquiescence, outbursts of anger, criminal behaviour. Because those people have no expectation of change whatsoever, and in fact have lost all self-confidence, nothing does change.

'The first stage towards overcoming this suffering', says Dorothee Sölle, 'is to find a language that leads out of the uncomprehended suffering that makes one mute – a language of lament, of crying, of pain, a language that at least says what the real situation is.' She sees the significance of liturgy and worship as being ways in which men can express themselves in their sorrow and pain and happiness. Prayer breaks through the barrier of dumbness and turns the mute God of apathy into the voice of the God of liberation. 'It was this God with whom Christ spoke in Gethsemane.' She sees the psalms as a phase in the process of change. 'I consider the stage of articulation, the stage of psalms, to be an indispensable step on the way to the third stage, in which liberation and help for the unfortunate can be organized.'[2]

Faith in the possibility of change is an essential ingredient in this process. A minimum of self-reliance is necessary. This word conveys two necessary aspects: the basic confidence that one is in a position to bring about change, and the possession of the means to achieve change. It is a matter of knowing one's own capacity.

The Bible testifies to the way in which the poor regain this capacity, both materially and spiritually. God recognizes their existence. They are not inferior beings; indeed they may delight in God's special favour. The life and work of Jesus represented a particularly strong stimulus to the self-reliance of the poor. First, of course, because Jesus himself was poor. He keeps no one at arm's length. His approach is in no way condescending: he does not offer charity. He meets men on their level. He attracts the outcasts and eats with the victims of social discrimination. He tells the weary and the heavy-laden to come to him and learn from him, because he himself is poor; in that way they will find rest for their souls. In other words, they will regain their self-reliance and discover and be able to accept and believe in the way of redemption. In this context, Gustavo Gutierrez speaks of spiritual childhood. It is to have no other food than to do the will of the Father who is in heaven (John 4.34).

Spiritual and material aspects overlap, but never in such a way as to provide the rich with an excuse. On the contrary, the rich man is required to adopt the same basic attitude as the poor man, caught up in his poverty. In this respect the poor man is at an advantage.

If the rich man has the same attitude as the poor man and becomes a spiritual child, living from the grace of God, then he can become detached from his possessions as he needs to be. In that case he will no longer rely on his possessions, but will have become independent of them. Because the poor man has no possessions, he is at an advantage in the kingdom of God. The rich man can only enter that kingdom when he has freed himself from his riches. And because this is so difficult, it is easier for a camel to go through the eye of a needle than for a rich man to enter the kingdom of God (Matt. 19.24 and parallel passages).

The imagery is a grotesquely humorous way of depicting how a man who is unprepared to put his cumbersome possessions aside will get stuck in the entrance to the promised kingdom. A harrowing prospect for those who realize that in our prosperous welfare states most of us cut the strangest capers in order to hang on to our possessions and yet at the same time remain within God's kingdom. The inevitable result is a Christian neurosis. It is no accident that in the Sermon on the Mount, in which the essential principles of the divine covenant are ratified and solemnly renewed, the poor receive the blessing. As I have already shown, there is a difference in the text between Matthew (the poor in spirit) and Luke (the poor). The difference is not as great as might seem at first sight. Obviously no one social class is canonized or beatified as such. Still less are those who are poor in this world's goods promised future blessings in heaven as a consolation prize, so that this earthly vale of tears vanishes in the heavenly glory to come. Gutierrez prefers an interpretation which puts poverty in a prophetic perspective. 'Blessed are they when the coming of the kingdom brings an end to their poverty and creates a brotherly world.' This seems to be a desperate expedient; even if it does not offer only a heavenly prospect, it is exclusively oriented on the future and only has future benefits to offer. Yet Jesus does not say that the poor will be blessed one day; they are blessed now. In both Matthew and Luke, the emphasis on the present is striking. The accent is on the word *is*: 'Yours *is* the kingdom of heaven' (Matt. 5.3); 'Theirs *is* the kingdom of God' (Luke 6.20).

In a delightful book,[3] a Dutch writer has shown how the difference between Matthew's phrase 'kingdom of heaven' and Luke's phrase 'kingdom of God' is connected with the difference between their audiences. Jewish readers were not allowed to utter the name of the Eternal. Both phrases are thus concerned with the kingdom, or rather, the kingly rule of God; even 'kingdom of heaven' is a present reality – not elsewhere, in the future. So the beatitude about the poor relates to their present state. What a good thing it is that you are poor, because that means that you are already included in this kingdom of God.

This statement is true of the poor by definition, and of the rich conditionally. The rich (including those who think themselves to be rich in faith) must be poor in spirit. And anyone who is poor in spirit can abandon all possessions. That will bring him blessing.

From apathy to liberation movements

This beatitude has a liberating effect on the poor man. It stirs him from his apathy, from his utter despair at the possibility of change. There he is, unable to speak, to complain or to resist, acquiescing dumbly in the inevitable. He has nothing to believe or to hope. And then this barrier is broken through.

Those concerned with economic development have come to see that, as in welfare work, help offered from a position of superiority, however well-intentioned, is useless unless there is some development from below. At a conference in Holland in 1977, the Indian economist Dr Samuel Parmar argued that the recipients of aid should themselves lay down the conditions on which help should be sent. He felt that the most important of these conditions was the possibility that the recipient could *refuse* the help offered. Aid must tie in with the plans of the recipients. They must be able to help themselves (possibly with the help of others). To be able to do that they have to believe in their own potentialities.

The fact that in Jesus a redeemer appears who is himself poor and pronounces blessings on the poor must not only have had a marked emotive attraction for the helpless and needy in Palestine; it will also have been a powerful stimulus. The poor were no longer the object of charity, however well-intentioned; they were at the centre of the move towards change and were themselves in a position to bring it about. The perspective from which the gospel is written takes the poor out of their isolation and gives them the support that they need. Furthermore, the proclamation of a crucified saviour ('Jesus Christ and him crucified', I Cor. 2.2) is not a slogan of orthodoxy; it is a provocative announcement that the Lord of the church is himself one of the outcast.

Redemption, reconciliation and liberation are not grounded in supremacy, in the oppressive superiority of the strong, but in the openness and self-surrender of this Jesus who refused to be rich, willing to stay utterly poor to the end. Consequently, his church is intended to be a church of poor people and slaves. The rich are welcome, but only if they are poor in spirit. This means that they will also need to become materially poorer, by serving in the community as one brother to another.

The story of the healing of a lame man in Acts 3.1–10 is a vivid example of this. On Yae Shik, a Korean from the Asiatic Institute of Church and Industry working in Japan, preached a sermon connecting this lame man with the countless people in our society who have been turned into beggars. Political propaganda and the distorted slogans of those in authority hold masses of people in their paralysing grip. All the talk of economic success does not help them one little bit. A beggar's hands have to be stretched out in humility and meekness. This is what the lame man did as he sat at the beautiful gate of the Temple. All his resources had been sapped. The flame of his vitality had been quenched. And what did Peter do? Give him money? That could have emphasized his inferiority and helplessness. Charity gives only superficial help. No, On Yae Shik argues, Peter freed the man from the slavery of misleading slogans. He did not give him any gold. 'I have no silver and gold.' He did not give him any power. What he did do, in the name of the Lord, was to rekindle the man's own vitality. 'In the name of Jesus Christ . . . walk.' Peter acted by rejecting existing patterns and practices. That was all he could do. He did not have much. All he had was his solidarity with and his faith in this preposterous redeemer. His was a weak, little voice which did not seem up to coping with the slogans of the time; however, it was enough to rekindle a force that was already in existence. Once revived, this force enables a man to walk on his own feet.

The name of Jesus spread like wildfire through the ancient world. His support for the poor, his own property, his openness, his cross and resurrection – tangible proof that God was on his side – brought into being a new community which could look for the impossible.

A booklet published in Holland in 1976 shows that the process of change begins with the arousing of expectations, and all the conflicts and oppositions to which it leads.[4] When apathy prevails nothing happens. 'When the slave is utterly convinced that everything happens in accordance with the will of the gods, and most people accept the existence of masters and slaves, as they accept the existence of birds and fishes, then society can have a long and fairly happy life.' But once people have a different picture of the world and believe in the possibility of change, they regain their self-confidence and press for change.

Jesus' celebration of poverty and his radical liberation of the poor, within the context of reconciliation, set in motion the wheels of change.

His liberation is profoundly spiritual. It comes about through his attractive spirituality, or – and this amounts to the same thing – through his holy spirit. In the midst of many disastrous fires, this Holy Spirit is itself a fire. It lights men up, arouses them from their dejection and gives them the courage they need, without causing the discord and division to which such inspiration can give rise. However, the knife has to be there. 'I have not come to bring peace, but a sword' (Matt. 10.34), Jesus says to his disciples.

The liberation brought about by Jesus is more than liberation from material poverty; however, that aspect is very much part of it. Liberation movements are certainly not manifestations of holiness, nor are they carried on by saints. However, Christians will be prepared to see them as evidence of the working of the spirit of Christ. They will also become involved, taking care that the end in view is *total* liberation, which calls for more than a change of circumstances. What is the point of the poor simply becoming rich?

Biblical spirituality is a necessary element in the process of liberation. It is concerned with total liberation, the discovery of God's man in God's world. That is why the Bible chooses the poor and the poor in spirit as the basis of the new kingdom of God, which is at the same time the kingdom of men.

7

Can even the Rich be Saved?

Righteousness, solidarity and spirituality are the words which sum up biblical opposition to poverty. Can they still be used in our time? Before we ask that, we must ask a more serious personal question. Can the rich be instruments of salvation?

The answer is, no.

The rich cannot be saved, nor can they bring salvation. That must be left to the poor. The basic biblical pattern is clear. In a world where justice has been lost and the covenant between men has been broken, the rich cannot put themselves forward as those who will make the world a better place while still retaining their riches. They cannot get a share in the salvation of the new kingdom all for themselves. Why should they? They already have their reward.

We are not concerned here with riches generally, as though being rich and prosperous were a bad thing. That is not the case. The Bible is not against enjoying the good things of the earth. But when some men are rich because others are poor, and when the prosperity of some is achieved at the expense of others, how is it possible for a rich man to be saved? His riches get in the way. They threaten to rob him of his soul and his salvation. How can injustice ever be a basis for blessedness?

There are various explanations of the difference in incomes throughout the world. There is no denying the fact that one of the causes lies in the attitude of the rich countries. It is our trade regulations, our use of raw materials, our prices and our power which see to it that most of the resources of the world are used to the benefit of those who are already rich, and not for those who have most need of them, in the developing countries. And what is true of external relations is also true at a deeper level. One still finds a constant underlying sense of hostility within societies, even if they have been as it were tamed and domesticated through an increasing amount of social legislation. The norm for our actions is not mutual solidarity, but the accumulation of personal possessions, regardless of the fact that this is at the expense of others.

Once when I was giving a talk about the World Council of Churches' programme to combat racism, I was attacked sharply by an industrial worker from Friesland. This is what he said. 'Why do you lay all this stress on racial conflict in the Third World? You seem to forget that we are living in a permanent state of class conflict here. Look at our houses. Who are the people who live in large comfortable houses? Who live in small workers' houses? Who live in the back streets with inadequate facilities? Who live in attractive suburbs?'

He was quite right to be irritated. My wide-ranging approach ignored actual problems closer to home and sounded like an evasion of this issue. I was so preoccupied with problems abroad that I had failed to reflect on my own salary, house and social position. I had given myself a progressive image by championing the poor abroad, and had not even seen any need to change my own social position.

Poverty and riches are relative words, and that makes things complicated. The poor here are rich in comparison with the poor in developing countries. Their relative wealth here is partly derived from oppression of the poor elsewhere. The money which the multi-national corporations bring into our countries also contributes to our general prosperity. As a result, the oppressed here become the exploiters elsewhere. We are all part of the same problem, some more than others.

The only solution is to put an end to any form of exploitation. The Bible is agreed on that. Charity may often be important, but the crucial word is justice. Once the rich man becomes concerned with justice, he can join in God's new order. Appeals from charities, sales of work and other fund-raising activities are marginal phenomena. The righteousness of the covenant requires something more, because it has more to give. It gives solidarity, unity within the covenant, unity between man and God, and unity among mankind. Consequently it looks for the restoration of unity, the reintegration of men and society. There is one interesting aspect to the message of the Bible which offers hope to us, who are more or less rich. The rich are not imprisoned in their riches. They can get out. They are never written off. They are never even regarded with jealousy. On the contrary, people feel sorry for them.

But they have the law and the prophets. That is their chance. They can become righteous, work for the restoration of justice, and learn to accept that for the Bible private property is never a right; property is always at the disposal of the community. To go back to the three terms we have been considering: the rich can become righteous, learn solidarity and become poor, if that is necessary for their salvation. They can become poor in spirit and – if need be – poor in possessions. So I propose to add some further comments on these three possibilities.

Becoming righteous

We are lucky to be living at a time and in a part of the world where questions of poverty and riches are already seen to involve justice rather than charity. And this insight has led to some change.

We have achieved a more equitable distribution of income. There have been many changes in the Western world, especially after the Second World War. People are concerned not only to make more money available for development in poor countries but also, increasingly, to remove the causes of underdevelopment, even if there are hesitations when our economy is affected. The church, too, is busy, although more among officials in senior positions than in local communities. In particular, the World Council of Churches is playing a prominent part.

When it comes to ecumenical action, life-style movements make it increasingly clear as they go on that the important thing is not to have a superficially better life but to reformulate the aims of society and rediscover the joy of living. What we do with our time, our money, our work and our possessions gives a clear indication of our concerns.

At the same time, some people do not hesitate to take a very critical view of their own society. Many of them are beginning to realize that the capitalist structure of our economy is getting in the way of human happiness. The vehemence of the opposition which develops here makes it clear on the one hand how attached we are to our possessions and on the other how keen we are for change. It is becoming increasingly evident that change here means change in the way in which factories and businesses are owned and run. The question of property is becoming more and more urgent. Our towns are full of empty houses, so attractive to the squatters who break into them, which are as untouchable as some sacred object. We do not need them as homes, but only as forms of investment. The church can no longer be separated from politics. In the Bible, the call for righteousness, God's love for us and ours for God, belong together in a way that we find most confusing. In a book like Deuteronomy, righteousness seems to have far-reaching consequences for personal possessions, just as in the same book love of God is a matter of life and death. Unity is to be found in the Lord God himself. 'Hear, O Israel, the Lord our God is one Lord' (Deut. 6.5). In the New Testament we can see how Jesus is opposed to any trend which might break up society or the church. His message is based on this oneness. The new kingdom is embodied in him. The year of jubilee dawns as he appears. The fact that he irrevocably chose to be poor saves the poor from the externalized interference of those who despise them or seek to help them, and gives a radical dimension to reintegration. The poor man does not need primarily to be helped. He is the rightful claimant, who is welcomed into the new kingdom as its heir. He has as much right to this world's goods as anyone else.

This growing insight in the churches initially brings frustration, and sometimes even has a paralysing effect. The reality of this world is diametrically opposed to such an incredible gospel. This is further emphasized by a strong trend in some Protestant circles where it is thought that blessing is reflected by material success. Moreover, for most of us, prosperity is a relatively recent phenomenon. A great many of us were brought up in an atmosphere of grim austerity and permanent shortage. Now that things are rather better, one can see how criticism of prosperity can be psychologically disturbing, especially when it comes from those who never lifted a finger to help the needy with their burdens. Only mutual understanding can provide a context for that pattern of frustration which is manifestly expressed in the Bible. It can be found throughout the gospels, in the sometimes vain struggle by the prophets against economic and political developments, and within the New Testament in the minority position of the church. This frustration may seem negative, but it can also have a creative effect. People are in search of new ways and sometimes they manage to find them.

The Bible is itself a history of this quest. The way chosen is not that of violent revolution, which in fact does no more than restore earlier conditions, but that of voluntary self-sacrifice, the cross. This self-sacrifice is the basis of the community's existence. So how can anyone who insists on clinging to his possessions, who allows himself to be ruled by mammon and acts unjustly, have any share in the kingdom? He has forfeited it in advance. By contrast, anyone who is prepared to lose his life, i.e. anyone who is willing to give up property, house, money, goods, family, himself, finds that he has gained everything.

The resurrection of Jesus proves that he is right. At the very point at which he lost everything and even had to sacrifice the one thing he did have, his life, he turned out to have won everything. The disruptive forces within his world did not succeed in getting the better of him. His followers found this a convincing demonstration that his way was a good one. It created an inter-relationship between men and things and God; in short, it brought salvation. This belief overcame their frustration and transformed their helplessness into creative initiatives. A tension remained between what has already taken place and the kingdom expected in the future: to begin with, in a very short time. It was impossible to do much more than make a start. A signpost could be set up here and there. Because they were a tiny minority group, Christians had to leave things at that.

In our day, however, Christians make up a third of the world's population. So, it ought to be possible to do more. Christians can no longer escape the question of what they do with their power. Metropolitan Paul Gregorios, the present leader of the Syrian Orthodox Church in India, and formerly known as Paul Verghese, has argued for the reintroduction of the year of jubilee. It might be best to replace a welfare state controlled by all kinds of organizations and government bodies with an open society based on trust in God. However unrealistic that might seem, to allow things to take their course could well be a better solution than any realistic model. His remarks appear in a book published by the World Council of Churches' Commission for the Churches' Participation in Development (CCPD). A later publication from this Commission (1975) tried to find ways through oppression and dependence towards a 'just and sustainable participatory society' – a phrase which has now become a standard expression within the World Council of Churches.

The Bible does not have a blueprint for what we should do. Our world is too different. What it does say, however, it says with some emphasis. Its fundamental conviction is that the world and everything in it is the Lord's, and that for a limited group of people to lay claim to the world's resources is sin. It is sin in respect of those who are despised, and sin for those who have too much; they lose their happiness, as we see from the example of so many people in our so-called welfare state.

The church should make a stand for the corporate use of possessions, the reintegration of society and the redistribution of the means of production. This amounts to a claim for righteousness and justice. The church should not hesitate to discuss the individuals right to property. On the basis of the unity of the covenant, it must encourage its members to claim justice at all levels of politics, in trade union activities, in national and international law and in relationships between workers. The church should not regret its own helplessness, or its own power. The church is helpless because there are no obvious solutions, and its symbol and foundation is the cross, not the clenched fist. It has power, because of its many members, and above all because of an authority which has been tested down the ages. It presents the claims of the poor and therefore has equality and the future on its side. At the least, that is the case when it heeds its prosperous and sometimes subversive message, a message which is subversive when it comes to something as sensitive as human possessions. Anyone who looks up the word property in a concordance will see at a glance how demanding the Bible can be:

'sold all that he had', 'was sad because he had many possessions', 'they responded by giving up all their possessions', 'sell all that you have', 'silver and gold have I none', 'Do not hold back any of your possessions', 'as having nothing and yet possessing all things'.

Among all the polarization in the world, the church will just have to be itself. When rich people are unwilling to give up their riches, and use them for selfish ends, it must proclaim and demand justice for the poor, one-sidedly and radically. And if there is no other way, its members will have to suffer and fight for that justice.

At the same time, individual members of the church, and sometimes the institutional church itself, will have to take part in liberation movements and social revolutions. It will have to make it clear that the replacement of one form of authority or regime by another will not solve the problem. Why should the new rich be any better than the old? The church is not concerned with revolution, but with conversion. It looks for complete change, and the end of all oppression. The church stands for justice because of the freedom it knows it has been given. This freedom acts as a stimulus and makes some things look relatively unimportant. Jesus dissociates himself from all kinds of possessions with an almost holy indifference. What advantage is it for a man if he gains

93

the whole world, but loses or harms himself (and his soul) (Matt. 16.26; Mark 8.36; Luke 9.25)? This question applies to both rich and poor, and indicates the principle of the new kingdom: total dedication to God's love and righteousness. That is possible only for those who can detach themselves from what they have – and live in the same way as the poor.

Learning solidarity

There is historical evidence to show that the attraction of the first community did not lie in its missionary campaigns (there is virtually no call to evangelize in any of the epistles), but in its way of life. Their very real brotherhood made Christ's community particularly attractive to a world which was so disrupted by social conflicts. If people could live like this, their God must be very special. Within a setting of this kind, words like God, reconciliation, love, grace, liberation found a real response. They were not seen as alien elements but as necessary explanations of human experience. Without pretentious verbal claims, and simply by the way in which it broke down the barriers of class, race and sex, the church became a healing power in society. In medical groups within the World Council of Churches there has been much thought and experimentation with the idea of the church as a 'healing community'. Bringing sick people into a group which lives by the gospel creates a climate in which they can be helped to think in terms of total restoration rather than simply of cure for their physical sickness.

Christ's community ought also to take the trouble to set up such 'healing communities' throughout the world in the socio-economic sphere as well. In them the spiral of greed could be broken and people could be invited to show solidarity with one another. Someone has to make a start in protesting against the commercialization of society which is overwhelming us like a flood and which we cannot cope with as individuals. The Christian community should make itself an attractive model of real sharing.

Development economists often speak of structural imperialism.

Underdevelopment is not just a consequence of external circumstances (poor and rich countries): it is also a consequence of internal factors (unjust conditions within the countries themselves). 'There are no poor countries,' said the Indian Christian economist Dr Sam Parmar in a lecture to the Free University of Amsterdam, 'but only countries where the conflict between the rich and the poor is greater or lesser.'

Within our own Western political systems there are spasmodic signs of a struggle between the strong and the weak, a selfish concern for one's own privileges. This is a fatal force, which turns people into competitors and constantly deceives the weak or reduces them to the consumer level. It can only be broken from within by deep conviction and firm belief. No one can do it by himself in what is becoming a totalitarian world. One becomes indifferent, or evades the demand in a variety of ways. Some people do this by disregarding and devaluing the material world and concentrating on a spiritual world apart from every-day reality. Others do it by making radical pronouncements which are not backed up by actions. The idealists of today become the disillusioned of tomorrow and cynics of the day after.

More than any other group, on the basis of its own experience of community, the church of Christ has every reason and every possibility for making a real contribution to the rediscovery and reconstruction of the society which God has in mind and which he will bring about in his own good time. As the 1976 Christmas letter from Taizé puts it: 'The people of God have unique possibilities to contribute towards this future; they are spread throughout the world, resolved to share all things with all men, and can stand as a symbol within human society.'

So far sharing has been limited to smaller groups, sects and orders. It is remarkable that so far as I know the organized church has never taken steps in this direction. All its initiatives, however admirable, have remained firmly in the sphere of welfare. Increasing attention has been paid to justice in foreign lands, but what really needs to be done just does not happen. During the week, people who address one another as brother and sister every Sunday seem to belong to conflicting groups. Whatever may be understood in theory, in practice things are very different. The unity of the church is affirmed verbally, but after Sunday worship, that goes by the board.

Not only has the church lost contact with the lowest social classes; in fact countless other people have never been accepted into its community. In practice, congregations often consist of a number of closed social classes and detached individuals.

Anyone who looks at levels of income within a congregation and discovers what some can spare and others cannot, will be very doubtful about talk of solidarity. The contribution of the parish towards helping the poor remains marginal. Equalization of income is left to the political parties, when the community itself could make a beginning here. Why does it not?

If the community is the basis for our solidarity, this is where it should be possible to break through the vicious circle. There is good reason why the desire for money is one of the sins which is condemned in the Bible at any period. It stands on the same level as adultery and theft.

So far I have said little about solidarity with the world outside. Perhaps we are still a long way from achieving that. But mutual solidarity is already so minimal, and is so hampered when it comes to questions of property, income and possessions, that here too new initiatives are necessary. Attitudes on these issues were what helped the first community to grow, and the church fathers for a long time regarded them as self-evident.

Can the rich be saved? No, unless they begin to learn this kind of solidarity. The learning process begins with the 'attention' about which Simone Weil has written: we must not shield ourselves from our neighbours' suffering, but allow our obligations and perplexities their full force. We must be open to others, not as bystanders, but as fellow human beings. We have to learn vulnerability in dealing with ourselves and others. In this context Dorothee Sölle speaks of prayer in which all isolation is done away with and men can once again become themselves before God. 'Therefore in industrial society, prayer is itself a subversive act.'[1]

Suffering can be echoed in prayer. It is no longer suppressed and driven to silence.

Here, too, the implications are clear. It is not a matter of replacing capitalism with socialism. What is the advantage, if this amounts to no more than a shift in control of the means of production? The important thing is to overcome the power of materialism. The community derives from its Lord the strength to be independent and can therefore experiment with patterns of fellowship. These experiments are more difficult than proclamations. They will come up against more opposition, but they will help. They will help the rich as well as the poor, in relieving them of the fear that they are insignificant unless they have possessions. Experiments in patterns of fellowship have a spiritual dimension.

Becoming poor

So can the rich be saved? No, unless they become poor in spirit. That is the way a catechism might put it. We are told that in AD 312, shortly before his decisive victory, Constantine the Great saw the sign of the cross in the clouds with the words *in hoc signo vinces*, 'in this sign you will conquer'. In the area in which I grew up, you could see this cross with the letter IHS shining out on the doors of Roman Catholic households. Winning and the cross belong together. The incredible had happened. The sign of the deepest humiliation had been elevated into the sign of the supreme power. And that point, according to many people, marked the end of Christianity. 'Woe to you rich' seemed once and for all to have been replaced by celebration of conquest.

Things are different in the Bible. There it becomes clear that the deepest cause of the conflict between rich and poor does not derive from external factors; it is essentially a matter of human anxiety. Power, money, possessions, other people, authority and love are necessary because there are those who feel that they are nothing without them. That is why the Bible is never sorry for the poor. It takes their side and pleads their cause. It is sorry for the rich. What a pity you are rich! Luke's 'woes' in chapter 6 of his gospel do not have moralistic implications. They are an expression of Jesus' pity. We say, 'What a pity about the poor!' Jesus says precisely the opposite. 'Blessed are the poor. What a pity about the rich!' The Greek simply says 'Alas'.

If as a church we live by the grace of God (and this is what we stress in our theology), and are not dependent on ourselves or on prestige and power, then we shall be able to undermine our society, which is based on prestige.

This is the point with which Matthew in particular is concerned. Luke came up against the real poor in his society, just as Paul kept coming up against the underdogs as he travelled round the Roman empire. Matthew was concerned with people who regarded themselves as the élite of the establishment, and who already had everything. To be able to enter the kingdom of God they had to learn to become poor, to stop relying on the Law, on their expectations, on their status: they had to learn to trust this strange suffering Messiah. That was their hope of salvation. For Matthew, the blessing is only for the poor in spirit and those who hunger and thirst after righteousness. Together with the meek, the sorrowful, the merciful, the pure in heart, the peacemakers, the persecuted and those who are reviled for Christ's sake, they belong to the kingdom of heaven.

This spirituality in no way minimizes or makes light of human need and suffering. It simply brings out the biblical perspective: which is not directed downwards from above, and is not concerned with charity and technology. It sees that the poor man himself must act on the basis of his own potential.

Luke himself has to concede that although their chances are slim, the rich can enter the kingdom of God. But if that is to happen, they will need God. And the Bible makes it clear that that can only mean conversion and living by God's grace. Those who do that will learn justice: they will stand alongside, rather than over, their fellow men. They will themselves become poor. Their possessions will no longer be the basis for their life nor a destructive power. They will become instruments capable of acting justly and rediscovering the joy of corporate living.

Study Suggestions

THE RICH, THE POOR — AND THE BIBLE provides a careful examination of the broad teaching of the Bible concerning poverty and riches. Many of the author's observations and insights differ starkly from the assumptions that widely prevail in Western society. It is therefore seriously recommended that this book be used as a resource for study, particularly by church officers and members, who are inevitably involved in the issues this book touches.

In a series of discussions the texts of the Bible, the contentions of the author, and the beliefs and assumptions of the class participants can meet in open encounter. With a desire to prove and challenge and explore, horizons can be lifted, conviction modified, and attitudes reformed.

The proposed outline is for a course of five sessions. There is nothing inspired about the number five. It appears that the contents of the book can be surveyed within that scheme, and the participants are more likely to commit themselves to five sessions rather than to a longer series. Only a series of questions are provided, with the intention that these may be helpful when it is necessary to open up the inquiry. Discussion leader and participants should have their Bibles handy, for it is in the light of God's word that the author's interpretations of the subject, as well as our own, should be tested.

I
Why Are Poor People Poor?
(Read Chapter 1)

1. What Bible verses can you cite that deal with the rich and the poor? From these verses, what attitude is shown toward the rich? the poor?

2. On a chalkboard or on a sheet of paper write the words "rich" and "poor." (Think of poor as those with less than an annual income of $4,000, in the United States, and the rich as those with more than an annual income of $50,000.) Under each, make a list of descriptive words and phrases.

   Compare the two lists.

   What do they suggest about our assumptions concerning the rich and the poor?

   Compare the terms you used with those the Bible uses to describe the person (pp. 7-10 in the text).

3. Give examples from biblical history and from modern times of how changing social conditions affect the number of the poor and society's attitude toward the poor. What conclusions can you draw from these examples as to why poor people are poor?

4. In what sense do you think people deserve what they get of this world's goods?

5. How would you respond to these statements by the author (p. 3)?

   "There is clearly an underlying connection between poverty and riches."

   "One person is poor because another is rich."

   "Poverty is no accident; it is determined by the structures of society."

6. Why are poor people poor?

II
Poverty in Ancient Israel
(Read Chapters 2 and 3)

1. The author states, "The question of poverty and riches seems hardly to play any significant role at all in earlier biblical literature" (p. 10). How can this be accounted for?
2. How did Israel's transition from a nomadic to an agrarian life following their settlement in Canaan affect their attitude toward ownership of property (pp. 13-15)?
3. In what way did the development of the army and the monarchy affect the economic and social life of the Israelites?
4. What effect did the exile have on Israel's basic socioeconomic structure?
5. Various texts of the Bible account for poverty in different ways — for example, laziness, destiny, or sin. How does one's assessment of poverty influence the way one responds to it?
6. In regard to the Bible's attitude toward poverty, the author asserts: "Poverty is never described calmly; it is challenged. . . . Reading the Bible is more dangerous than we often would like it to be. It puts us under an obligation" (p. 29). What obligation?

III
God and the Poor
(Read Chapter 4)

1. In what way did the Torah require justice for the poor?
2. What do these provisions in the law indicate about God's attitude toward the poor and the oppressed?
3. How do you account for the prophets' intemperate attacks upon the rich? Are their criticisms personal or against the rich as a group?
4. How do the writers of the New Testament compare with the prophets in their attitudes toward the rich?
5. What place has the covenant in defining the basic relationships

between persons? in determining the fundamental structures of society?

6. The author states, "The gospel is written from the perspective of the poor man" (p. 50). Do you agree? What difference does it make?

7. What contribution can the Christian community make to reform a society whose structures deprive and oppress?

IV
A Caring Community
(Read Chapter 5)

1. In what ways do differences in income threaten the unity of a family? Where does one expect and usually find help when hardship or disaster strikes? What is the basis of mutual caring and concern?

2. Why is lack of concern and actual exploitation of persons particularly to be condemned among God's people?

3. To what degree is it realistic to share what one has with others in need? How can you determine when you have done enough?

4. What hope is there for a rich person to enter the kingdom?

5. What distinguishing qualities mark the genuine fellowship of God's people?

6. In what ways can the believing community best influence the society in which it exists to respond supportively to those in need?

V
The Blessed Poor
(Read Chapters 6 and 7)

1. What would you consider to be the poor person's greatest need?

2. If it is, as the author suggests, "to be rescued from his feelings of separateness, inferiority and self-contempt" (p. 77), how did these become the greatest needs?

3. What would you consider to be the rich person's greatest need?

4. If it is to be relieved of the fear "that they are insignificant unless they have possessions" (p. 97), how did this come to be?
5. Why are well-intended gifts of charity often resented by those to whom they are given?
6. What can be done to restore a person to self-reliance?
7. If being rich and prosperous is not a bad thing, why does the author insist that "the rich cannot be saved, nor can they bring salvation. That must be left to the poor" (p. 87)?

Notes

Chapter 1 (*pp. 1–6*)

1. A. Gélin, PSS, *Les pauvres que Dieu aime*, Paris 1967, Appendice 1, Essai bibliographique. This survey describes exegesis in the period between 1882 and 1965. In this sympathetic and thorough book the author does not entirely avoid the temptation to praise poverty as a specific form of holiness.

2. In addition to the illustrations given above, see the list of 'misused' texts in G. F. Gilmore, 'The Bible on the Poor', in *Justice Rolling Like a River*, Commission on the Churches' Participation in Development (CCPD), WCC, Geneva 1975.

3. These considerations play an important role in the debate on development. There are those who look for economic growth as a basis for prosperity (the prosperity of the West needs only to trickle down to the poor countries and everything will be all right). Others are more concerned with just relationships and want to politicize aid, while a third group lays stress on men themselves as a basis for development (self-reliance). As is well known, since the conferences at Montreux in 1970 and 1974, the CCPD has preferred economic growth on the basis of justice and the independence of those concerned (self-reliance). This trio (justice, self-reliance and economic growth) is the basis for society in the so-called developed countries as well as in the so-called under-developed countries. Since the Assembly of the World Council of Churches at Nairobi in 1975, the favourite expression has been a 'just and sustainable participatory society'.

4. F. Belo, *Lecture matérialiste de l'évangile de Marc*, Paris 1975; S. Rostagno, *Essays on the New Testament, A 'Materialist' Approach*, WSCF, Geneva 1976. We shall return to the 'materialistic' method later in this book, and especially to the question whether this approach from much later times can be applied to the biblical texts. It will become clear

that any interpretation of a text from a distant age must work with modern terms and thus runs the risk of doing violence to it. In a way, translation is always betrayal.

5. Thus Emilio Campi in his preface to Rostagno's *Essays*, p. 6. This method also holds for the Old Testament.

Chapter 2 (*pp. 7–26*)

1. See the title of the book by O. Noordmans, *Zondaar en bedelaar* (*Sinner and beggar*), Amsterdam 1976.

2. See C. T. Kurien, *Poverty and Development*, Madras 1974, p. 6: 'Neutral economics is very much the ally of the rich and the powerful against the wretched and the oppressed.' It is therefore right for the church to oppose a neutral approach to the question of development.

3. It is strange that *ptochos* occurs ten times in the gospel of Luke, but not at all in his second book, Acts.

4. In Homer, riches consist in the possession of power and children; it is a matter of being blessed by the gods with a happy life. In this way the possession of material riches and their function are dissociated. Material riches are a benefit in themselves, quite apart from 'spiritual' riches. Aristotle and Plato go further, and combine riches with wisdom as something to be used for building up the *polis*, society. Later philosophers, the cynics, make this insight more radical. Poverty and not riches helps men to become wise. Poverty is the road to wisdom. Riches are corruption and an enemy to virtue. For the Stoics, possessions do not have any intrinsic value: the question is what one does with them.

5. See P. Humbert, 'Le mot biblique "*ebyon*" ', in *Révue d'histoire et de philosophie religieuses*, 1952, pp. 1–6. *Ebyon* does not appear in a number of strata of the Pentateuch; it is missing from the Yahwist, the Elohist and the Priestly writing, and the so-called Deuteronomistic history work (the books of Deuteronomy, Joshua, Judges, Samuel and Kings), though it does occur in the story of Hannah (I Sam. 1 and 2).

6. J. L. Koole, *De Tien Geboden*, Baarn 1964, pp. 85f.

7. For the role of Joseph in this see Gen. 47.13–26, a role which certainly will not have earned him people's thanks.

8. R. de Vaux, *Ancient Israel*, Darton, Longman and Todd 1964, p. 68.

9. But see the influential book by G. von Rad, *Old Testament Theology*, Vol. 1, SCM Press 1975, pp. 15–68. Von Rad speaks of the crises due to the conquest and the formation of the state.

10. A. Gélin, PSS, *Les pauvres que Dieu aime*, p. 12.

11. See André Gunder Frank. Among other works he has written *Capitalism and Underdevelopment*, New York 1967. His theory, which is open to some dispute, was developed in Latin America. He explains the contrasts in this world in terms of the shift of economic values from the periphery to the centre. Thus the developing nations are the periphery of the central developed nations (USA, Western Europe), while in the developing nations, the great cities drain the country. The centres make the periphery dependent on them.

12. C. T. van Leeuwen, *Sociaal besef in Israel*, Baarn n.d. (This is an abbreviated version of a dissertation produced in French under the title *Le Développement du sens social en Israël*).

Chapter 3 (pp. 27–30)

1. Gustavo Gutierrez, *A Theology of Liberation*, SCM Press 1974.

Chapter 4 (pp. 31–65)

1. Only foreigners have to pay interest. The righteous man does not exact any interest (Ps. 51.5), but the evil man does (Prov. 28.8; Ezek. 18.8, 13, 17). Interest in surrounding countries could amount to between 20% and 35%. Later (at the beginning of the Christian era) it dropped to 12%. As a result of these regulations a banking system in Israel was late in developing. Similarly, the level of interest exacted by money-lenders in Israel in early times is also unknown, but it will not have been very different from that exacted in the countries around Israel. For more detailed information see R. de Vaux, *Ancient Israel*, pp. 170f.

2. For the sabbath year and the year of jubilee see also the book by the Mennonite John Howard Yoder, *The Politics of Jesus*, Eerdmans, Grand Rapids 1972, which gives a detailed account, including subterfuges for evading the law, like the *prosboul*. Anyone who had debts to collect would often hand over his rights to the judge before the sabbath year or the year of jubilee. After the free year, the judge would then restore the original rights, which in effect meant that nothing changed. Hillel, an important rabbi from the time before Jesus, says, 'Give your demands to the judge and he will collect them for you (the *prosboul*).' Jesus says: 'Pay back before they bring you before the judge.' And to

the lender he says, 'Lend without hoping to get anything back' (Luke 6.35). According to Yoder (pp. 69ff), these rules meant that financial transactions stagnated. People would borrow whatever they could before the sabbath year or the year of jubilee.

3. The church fathers associate the name Cain with words like possessions and envy. In this way Cain becomes the embodiment of the church fathers' maxim: possessions are always sin. According to Martin Hengel, *Property and Riches in the Early Church*, SCM Press 1974, pp. 3ff., this notion of private property as the root of human discontent is an idea that permeates the social ethics of all the church fathers.

4. In particular I am thinking of the discussion between the 'liberation theologians' from Latin America and Western theologians like J. B. Metz and J. Moltmann (see, for example, the two articles by R. L. Haan, 'Moltmann in Buenos Aires', in *Gereformeerd Weekblad*, Nov./ Dec. 1977, published by Kok, Kampen).

5. Herman Ridderbos, *De Komst van het Koninkrijk*, Kampen 1950.

6. C. T. van Leeuwen, *Sociaal besef in Israel*, p. 48.

7. See especially R. E. Prothero, *The Psalms in Human Life*, John Murray 1903.

8. See the article by K. Dronkert, 'Liefde en gerechtigkeit' (Love and Righteousness) in *Schrift en Uitleg*, Festschrift for *W. H. Gispen*, Kampen 1970.

9. See J. M. Bonino, *Christians and Marxists*, Hodder 1976.

10. C. W. Mönnich, *De Koning te rijk*, Baarn 1975, p. 40.

11. See Hans-Rüdi Weber, *The Invitation: Matthew on Mission*, Joint Commission on Education and Cultivation, Board of Missions of the United Methodist Church, New York 1971, 42–44.

12. John Howard Yoder, *The Politics of Jesus*, p. 66.

13. See M. Hengel, *Property and Riches*, pp. 26ff.

14. There are even clear traces of apocalyptic, a viewpoint which was particularly prominent among the Jewish people from about 165 BC to AD 90. Here future and present are closely connected and initiates can know the language in which God's history is presented and work it out for themselves. In Mark 13, Matthew 24 and Revelation we find obviously apocalyptic terms, with lines going back to Daniel, Ezekiel, Zechariah and Joel. Terms like 'the beginning of the woes' and the use of symbolic language (dragon, snake, leviathan) derive from this pattern. In Jesus' words, talk about the last things does not involve this kind of calculation. He puts the dominant expectation in proper proportion

(Matt. 24.36). He turns it into responsibility for the present, and care for one another (Mark 13.33–37; Matt. 24.25–51).

15. H. Ridderbos, *Paul*, SPCK 1977, p. 316.

16. Ibid., p. 317.

17. M. Hengel, *Property and Riches*, pp. 9f.

18. For this interpretation see S. Rostagno, 'Is an Inter-class Reading of the Bible legitimate?' based on I Cor. 1.26–31. This article is included in *Essays on the New Testament, A 'Materialist' Approach*, WSCF, Geneva 1976. Rostagno is a representative of the materialistic interpretation of the Bible. One of the best-known advocates of this approach is F. Belo (see above), *Lecture matérialiste de l'évangile de Marc*, Paris 1975.

19. M. de Jonge, *Jezus, inspirator en spelbreker*, Nijkerk 1971.

Chapter 5 (*pp. 66–75*)

1. A. Gélin, *Les pauvres que Dieu aime*, p. 22.

2. In addition to Martin Hengel, *Property and Riches*, see A. Hamman OFM and S. Richter OFM, *Riches et pauvres dans l'Eglise ancienne*, 1962.

3. When famine threatened in Jerusalem in the 40s, Paul called for a great collection from the 'daughter churches'. The missionary church (Jerusalem) was poor and the mission churches were rich. Paul thought there was a fair exchange here. The spiritual riches of the one were counterbalanced by the material contributions of the other. Aid here, then, was truly reciprocal; the mission churches were not doubly dependent, as in our situation. The collection for Jerusalem has never been cited once as a plea for continued financial action in the moratorium debate or the question of mutual assistance. Here, however, the collection for Jerusalem is a bad example, because the roles are reversed; the poor missionary church is financially dependent on a richer area of mission – an ideal situation for missionaries. Paul's concern for equality should not be forgotten in the mission and evangelization of the church. Benefactors make bad missionaries.

Chapter 6 (*pp. 76–86*)

1. Dorothee Sölle, *Suffering*, Darton, Longman and Todd 1975, pp. 61ff.

2. Ibid., pp. 70, 78, 74.
3. F. Boerwinkel, *Meer dan het gewone*, Baarn 1977, p. 56.
4. R. V. A. Röling, *Armoede en oerlogsproblem*, IKV 1976.

Chapter 7 (pp. 87–98)
1. Dorothee Sölle, *Suffering*, p. 74.

Index of Biblical References

Luke		Acts		Philippians	
6	97	3.1–10	23, 84	2.7	50
6.20	1, 83	4.32	57		
6.21	40, 46, 47	4.32–37	58	**Colossians**	
6.24f.	37, 39, 47	5.1–11	58	3.11	54
6.30	52	5.4	58		
6.35	108	11.17	75		
7.22	39	18.8	73	**I Timothy**	
7.23	51			5.3–16	71
7.34	53			6.9f.	71
8.14	39	**Romans**		6.10	56, 57, 79
9.25	94	16.23	73		
9.58	49			**Titus**	
10.8	53			2.11	74
12.13–21	37	**I Corinthians**			
12.15	39	1.5	55		
12.21–23	39	1.16	73	**Hebrews**	
12.22–32	52	1.26	55, 73	11.13	12
12.23	2	1.26–31	109		
14.33	39	1.28	55		
14.35	46	2.2	84	**James**	
16.9	39	2.6	62	1.18	58, 63
16.10–12	39	7	54	2.1–13	56
16.13	44	7.29ff.	54	2.5–9	37
16.19–31	37, 48	11.20	55	2.6	39
18.18–27	37	11.29	55	2.7	73
18.22	48	15.24	62	4.13–17	37
18.25	39	16.15,17	73	5.1	39
18.27	39			5.1–6	37, 57
John		**II Corinthians**			
2.16	14	8.8	54	**Revelation**	
4.34	81	8.9	71	13.16	39
16.33	1	8.14f.	74	18.10	39
18.36	1f.			18.23	39
				18.24	39
Acts		**Galatians**		21.10	74
2.42–47	58	3.28	54	21.16	84
2.44	57	6.11	72		

112